Mum & Dad's War

Barbara Laws

Spire Books

South Barn, Old Standlynch Farm,
Downton, Salisbury SP5 3QR

Copyright © 2019 Spire Books, and
Barbara Laws
All rights reserved.
CIP data: a catalogue record for this book is available
from the British Library.

Designed by John Elliott

ISBN 978-1-904965-59-6

Contents

1	Introduction	5
2	Blackpool, February 1941	13
3	Southend on Sea, April 1941	31
4	28 April 1941	43
5	Hunsdon Nr Ware, 3 September 1941	65
6	From Hunsdon to Leicester, 1942	89
7	Moving to Bolton, June 1942	99
8	Move to SHQ Signals Section, RAF Duxford, Nr Cambridge, Sept 1942	113
9	Move to Babraham	117
10	Babraham continued 1943	143
11	Move to Gransden, Bedfordshire, April 1943	153

12	Move to Warboys, Mid-June 1943	165
13	Still at Warboys, 1944	185
14	Chelmsford, September 1944	211
15	Return to Warboys, September 14th	213
16	Course at Cranwell, November 1944	217
17	Return to Warboys, late November 1944	219
18	Still at Warboys, 1945	227
19	Wireless couse at Farnborough, 21 January 1945	231
20	Return to Warboys, 29 January 1945	233
21	Postscript	255
22	Manston airfield, 1946	261

1
Introduction

It was when clearing out their garage in 2017 that I came across a large box, entitled 'Economics lectures' and discovered a treasure trove of letters written between 1939-48. The more I delved into it, the more I realised that this correspondence not only charted the development of a friendship which was to lead to marriage in 1945, but it also chronicled the story of ' an ordinary war' as experienced by two young people who remained in England throughout the hostilities. So often war is glamourised, when the reality is humdrum. These letters gave me an insight into what it was really like to be in the RAF as ground staff, moving from drome to drome, trying to fit in with others of a different disposition, longing for weekend passes and leave and seeking meaningful social contact outside of the camp, whenever possible. I learnt what made my parents tick, what built them up and sustained them throughout a period of 7 years. I understood more about their

Introduction

hopes and fears, their interests and activities, their social network and their two respective families. In this book I hope to extract some of the essence of their 'ordinary war', which no doubt echoes the experience of many other young couples of that time and also to celebrate the positive influence which they have had upon my life as a result of those formative experiences.

Where to begin? Dad, (David Laws) grew up in the coalmining town of Barnsley, having been born in 1920 to parents who themselves had got married at the end of the First World War. His father was in charge of the administration and accounts at a colliery supplier and ironmonger's firm, Lawrence's. Outwardly a strict man, who was church organist and choirmaster, Ben Laws had a wicked sense of humour underneath and was much loved by his family. Dorcas Laws was a strong minded, determined, hard working mother who made the family her priority and set high standards for all to follow. They had three children, David (1920), Mary (1924) and Helena (1930), all of whom were fortunate to receive a grammar school education.

Mum (Eileen Laws/née Holland) grew up on a dairy farm in Billingborough, Lincolnshire. Her father (George Holland) was always busy milking the cows or going to market, whilst her mother (Daisy) stayed at home running the household, making butter and involving the children in local activities which seemed to centre around the Methodist church. There were 3 children, Eileen (born 1921), Dulcie (1924) and Norman (1927). Eileen too was lucky to get a scholarship at Donington Grammar School to which she travelled 6 miles daily on

Introduction

a service bus. Both David and Eileen left school with Matric, but opportunities for training were very limited at that point. David would like to have studied languages at university and Eileen would like to have gone to a domestic science college, but their parents advised them instead to go into the Civil Service as a 'safe' option for the future. David was very keen on the German language and in the summer of 1937 he had his German pen-friend, Walter, over to stay, taking him also on the family holiday to Filey. There was to have been a return exchange visit in the September 1938, but with the annexation of Austria, David's parents suddenly decided against his going to stay with a German family, however friendly and well-meaning they might be. It was one of his greatest regrets not to have managed this trip, but he retained a life-long interest in the language and after the war did resume some correspondence with Walter, although sadly they never managed to meet in person. So it was that David ended up at Louth Tax Office in 1937 and Eileen in 1939.

Their lives prior to leaving home had been relatively sheltered and financially secure. Codes of behaviour had been very much shaped by their experience of church and chapel. David had been a server at his local Church of England church and a letter from his former priest refers to this in 1935

> "This morning I received St Mary's magazine and I noticed your name down as a Server at St. Paul's, so I felt I must write you a line to tell you how delighted I am. It is a very great privilege to be able to assist the priest when he is celebrating at

Introduction

the altar in the most wonderful service that has ever been instituted, and at my church here I am very particular whom I ask to be server because I will only have the best. I always hoped you would serve at St. Paul's Altar and if I had remained with you longer I should have asked you, so now you will know how delighted I am. Try always to be worthy of it and to live your life during the week as a good and faithful soldier of Christ so that He may be pleased to see you kneeling before the Throne of God at that great Sacrament of the Altar. God bless you, my dear David, and I wonder whether you know how pleased I was to have the privilege and joy of preparing you for Confirmation. Give my love to your Father and Mother and Mary and little Helena. Your affectionate friend. Wilfrid Pawson."

Eileen's experience of chapel had been a bit more fun, in that she enjoyed the Sunday school anniversary celebrations, processing around the village and singing, but she too was expected to attend every week and observed her father's strong Methodist principles in action. I mention this because it forms the backdrop to understanding many of their wartime letters and appreciating why initially RAF life outside the cocoon of home seemed so alien. Although David had left home to go to Louth at the age of 17, he was cushioned from too harsh a reality because he found digs with a landlady and her husband, Mr. and Mrs. Lancaster, who effectively became substitute parents to him. Interestingly, he always refers to her as 'Mutti Lanc' and because she had no children of her own, she refers to him as 'Soehnchen' (little son) in one of her letters. She had a tremendously

Introduction

outgoing, positive and nurturing personality which people naturally warmed to and she was clearly a great homemaker.

1939 had been a strange year with threats of war and attempts at appeasement by Chamberlain. Eileen had a French pen-friend who sent a letter in May 1939, explaining quaintly about an old dance which had been adapted in France. It was called 'la Chamberlaine', based on the umbrella of Mr. Chamberlain. "Each dancer dances with his partner; one of them is alone and has an umbrella on his arm. He chooses a partner and takes it so he gives his umbrella to the dancer who searches for another partner. This dance existed before, but at the place of the umbrella this was a broom; this dance was danced only in family."

The gentility of this image was soon to be dashed by the outbreak of war in September 1939. Eileen had left home in July 1939 and fortunately she too found good digs outside of Louth in the village of South Elkington. She writes home "Well, I expect you will be anxious to know how I'm getting on; I have settled down well and feel perfectly at home with the Musgraves; Joan is very nice indeed and I think we shall become good pals. My bed is a feather one on top of a mattress and is very comfortable. The meals are very nice here and I still get my early morning cup of tea." Of her first day at the office she is equally positive and refers obliquely to David by saying. "There is one boy at the office, he took me to the station to collect my bike, as he has digs quite near there; he seemed quite nice he is a tax clerk and seems to do quite advanced work and telephoning

Introduction

etc." Little did they know that their world was about to explode – in more ways than one! Her first letter home had been so full of confidence and promise. She had landed a permanent job with two weeks' holiday pay, a pension and no superannuation to pay. Everything sounded secure. A village garden fete is mentioned along with tennis tournaments and horse racing. Her new driving licence had arrived and she concludes by saying "you need not worry at all about me, I'm quite OK and kicking, in fact it's an adventure which so far has been all right everywhere and I'm sure I shall like it because everyone is so jolly." Two months later war is declared.

Both David and Eileen continued to work, as normal, for the remainder of the year. He was a Tax Officer and she a Clerical Assistant. All I know of their original attraction to one another is that he would catch her eye across the desk and then swing a pulley for one of the electric lights towards her to gain her attention. By the Christmas of that year. there was an exchange of Xmas chocolates which David acknowledges in a formal thank you letter signed "Yours, very sincerely" whilst she writes "Cheerio and a happy New Year from Eileen". Each of them went home to their respective families for the holiday break and there was talk of a dance on 4th Jan 1940. Eileen took home a photo of David which she was brave enough to put up on the sideboard, but beyond this little is known of the early days of their friendship.

It was 1940 which seems to have been the year in which they really began to get to know one another, involving themselves in Louth activities such as the tennis club and amateur dramatics. Eileen became a Brownie leader and it seems David had a go at Sunday school teaching. Films and dances were the order of most weekends when both were in Louth together, but Eileen used to go home every other weekend by bus because her mother missed her so much.

In the February Eileen contracted German measles, which someone at the office commented wryly was "a Nazi thing to have." She had to be signed off work and it was at this point that a correspondence began. Oranges, which were a delicacy, began to be delivered to a new address where she was staying more centrally. David would cycle round and hover below her window, but he was not allowed to visit. By a month later she was back at South Elkington, but still in bed. She writes "I think it's awfully nice of you both (i.e. Mutti Lanc and David) to offer to come up and see me, but I'm afraid it won't be possible, as I shall only be allowed up for one hour in the afternoon and in addition I have not to get at all excited!" Easter came and went.

The friendship was still going strong by August 1940 when Eileen was corresponding from her summer holiday at home. The war did not seem to be impinging too much on life, in that she refers to croquet and tennis matches and outings to places of interest within Lincolnshire. Picnics are the order of the day. David writes "You really will enjoy it when you come to Grimoldby - particularly the croquet. It was very quiet at night also and there were very few planes about. Mrs. Lanc and I cycled over to the aerodrome and saw about 40 – all different types - spread over the field, looking

Introduction

as harmless as mechanical toys." The quiet before the storm.

By Christmas 1940, however, there was looming over them an abrupt end to civilian life, as men were being called up to join the forces. David spent Christmas with the Lancasters and New Year with his own parents. On 26th December he writes "I have just seen a poster about a New Year's Eve Dance – 8-2 [at the] Town hall - Old and modern dances and many surprises. Will you come? It might not be possible to go to another. Do say you will go and write to Barnsley from Billingborough." He must have known he was joining the RAF, because in the same letter he writes "By the way, Mrs. Robinson gave me 3 Air Force blue handkerchiefs and Nan gave me 6 with wings and RAF at the corner of each. And you remember that tie we saw in Cheers which you didn't like? Mrs. Lanc has given me that! I rather like it." As it was, Eileen initially declined the dance, but more on the grounds that she felt his family would be upset if he left them earlier than necessary and presumably no-one knew quite when the next leave would be. As it happened, he did make the dance because it was not until February that he was called up.

2
Blackpool, February 1941

The year 1941 ushers in a completely different scene. David has been moved to Blackpool for a period of general induction and square bashing. He sounds to be in a state of shock and isolation when he first arrives. He writes:

> "It is grand to have you to write to – my loneliness seems to vanish and I feel that if only I shut my eyes and put out my hand, yours will be there. When I wrote earlier in the afternoon, I could hardly hold my pen as I felt so scared and anxious, but with the events which happened since then, and the writing of a long letter home and now this letter, I feel very settled and much less worried. Really letter writing is marvellous for one. After I had posted your letter I returned and found a new chap had arrived - wireless operator – age 19, smokes, but does not drink and

Blackpool, February 1941

is a quiet type of fellow. He shows a definite desire to be friendly and as we both feel blue, we are sticking together - we have both to report to the same place tomorrow. The billet is not so bad. The fellows are a nice crowd and say the food is very good - they have had 3 eggs in 3 days - the room where I'm writing has a fire in and is as big as an ordinary living room and has 2 nice fireside chairs and a couch in it. We have our meals in here. It needs wallpapering etc., but the main thing it is comfortable. After tea Alf, the newly found friend, walked around with me in the Winter gardens and then to the Tower. We went in the latter, looked at the Aquarium, the Menagerie and went into the ballroom where a band was playing – Eileen! - you never saw such a beautiful ballroom – with plush chairs to sit on – two balconies (rather like cinema circles) and all done in gold, with magnificent lighting. I should love to take you there and perhaps I may sometime get the chance – it was only 1/2d for the whole lot and in uniform it is only 8d. I danced one waltz rather clumsily in big shoes and tried to imagine the eyes were blue and that her hair was curly instead of straight. Hope you won't call me silly, but in this last outpost, where one can be so lonely among so many, I do miss you more than ever. I have some photos, but am looking forward to receiving a proper one in your dance dress. I shouldn't bother now about a big one. This billet is quite comfortable and I have a nice fireside chair with a good fire. There are 3 other fellows here who are quite decent. The others have gone out to pubs and night club places. There is a tremendous amount of small talk here. The fellows are either grumbling about something they have done or got to do, or else

Blackpool, February 1941

> are swearing and talking about women in a nasty sort of way - they seem to forget that their own mothers and sisters are women. It makes me feel ill and it is at these times I feel most lonely. I try to shut my ears and if I am not actually doing something, I think about good things at home and at Louth and about good people like you and Mrs Lanc".

He goes on to explain that he has failed the medical because of having a perforated ear which will disqualify him from becoming a wireless operator. The remaining choice may be either an armourer or a clerk in accounts. One good thing is his uniform "I have a nice kit – a well-fitting tunic and two pairs of trousers." And he concludes by saying "Must stop now – I have my buttons to clean – bother it". He manages to phone his father for advice and the suggestion is to go for armourer "either learning to load up bombs or attend to guns on planes, as clerks may eventually be weeded out into infantry or any old job".

Eileen obviously realises that David is a bit out of his depth socially and is quick to put him in touch with one of her male cousins who was working nearby. They meet up and go for walks together. He also locates a female cousin who is 19, but whom he has only met twice before. "She is a nice sort of girl, interested in Sunday school work and table tennis at the church club. She is not flighty and can dance a little. She said next Friday at the Winter gardens is old time dancing, so I have arranged to take her - it is so much better with someone you know." Forming networks of trusted people will be one of the main ways in which David learns to make his

Blackpool, February 1941

wartime experience bearable and it seems that every time he is posted to a new place, somebody points him in the direction of a helpful, trustworthy person or group. But what was he actually doing each day in Blackpool? He recounts his routine as follows: "Yesterday morning we had foot drill and marching about for 2 ½ hrs. Then we were dismissed until 1.30 p.m. for inoculation - Typhoid and also vaccination. When this was done, we were sent home and told to go to bed early with 3 Aspros – the stuff makes your arm very stiff and as it gets around your body, you get all shivery - just like an attack of flu. Alf and I were in bed by 8.00 p.m. and perspired very much. We are allowed to have all today off to get over it and we got breakfast in bed - one of the corporals brought it up."

Eileen, on hearing how cold he is generally, knits him a scarf, bakes him a cake and comments in her next letter "I can't help thinking what a queer world this is. You seem to have been lifted by a Gulliver right out of one life and plonked down into an entirely different one." He outlines what is to happen "Today we were on parade at 8.15 a.m., received identity discs and an RAF identity card and the medical rejects like myself were placed in a special squad. We finished at 11.15 and were on this afternoon from 1.45-3.15 p.m., so we have not done so bad today. It is very reasonable, isn't it? We have had only one warning – Monday night - there was a deuce of a bang and planes were about, but we were all in bed, stewing with inoc. I feel that to be turned down for W/O is for my own good and that they are considering me - wireless may have ruined my ears

Blackpool, February 1941

which are very sensitive. I do not feel angry with them—in fact I am rather grateful for their careful examination." Unsurprisingly he goes down with a rotten cough and cold not long after his arrival in Blackpool, but over time the sea air does him good and the exercise makes him hungry. His mother visits from Barnsley and they go to a pantomime together, so he is not completely isolated. But he does refer to being in the 'Legion of lost souls' because of being a medical reject and being sent to South Shore, Blackpool. He draws his thoughts together in a carefully composed letter dated 12.2.41.

> "Dearest Eileen
> I have been thinking about you since leaving Louth and I feel I cannot let another moment pass without saying what I couldn't bring myself to say in words yesterday. I want you to know how much I appreciate and wish to thank you for your loyal companionship and friendship during the past 20 months. I feel this parting very greatly, as I have never before had such a pal as you, - a pal with whom I could share pleasures, happiness and sorrows and to whom I felt I could turn and confide in to any extent. Twenty months is a long time in some ways, but in a friendship such as ours, I feel it is a very brief period. We are but on the threshold of being very great friends. This parting will be good for us both. As you have already said, we are still very young and have many more people to meet and friends to make. In the meantime, until we do meet again, I shall go into this new life in the knowledge that I have in you a firm friend and that we are both praying for each other's safety amid so many dangers and

Blackpool, February 1941

> God's guidance in our friendship. So smile in the same old way (with that little wrinkle I know so well) and be brave at all times. Let me give you the little quotation Mrs Lancaster (bless her) gave to me: It is not life that matters, but the courage you bring to it. At the office, carry on in your usual way. I am sure you have a decent job coming to you, so when you get it, take it quietly and confidently and you will succeed. I say 'quietly' because I remember whenever I used to start on a nicer, but more difficult job, I used to get panicky and worried and all quite needlessly! Study hard between now and April and you will feel very confident. Now here's wishing you a Happy Birthday and a very pleasant time when you are at home and thank your mother on my behalf for the good wishes contained in her letter to you the other day.
>
> Goodbye, little pal, for the present.
>
> David."

It seems as if they had made a pact to think of one another every night at 10.30 p.m. and always to offer up a little prayer for guidance and safety. This practice continued throughout the war years. The war was becoming more real day by day. Back at the office the windows had been blacked out with scrim and there was a place to go in the event of an air raid. She writes a letter on 23rd February, describing how there was a descent of planes over Louth which led to her hiding under her desk, but a colleague yanked her out and took her to the filing/bundle room. She jokes that it was a

Blackpool, February 1941

good thing Mrs Lanc was not in the cake shop at this time. It seems that by now Eileen was actually lodging c/o the Lancasters, partly because South Elkington was a bit far out in the winter and the roads were very dark, even in the centre of town. With some of the men having gone into the forces, the office was now having to employ female temporary staff and Eileen was being asked to undertake new work, rather than just filing. She mentions half yearly assessments and Claims work, but it seems there was very little training for these new tasks and so she had to read instruction books in the evenings to understand what she was supposed to be doing. Some of the correspondence with David is seeking guidance and advice on how to approach various tax problems, but he obviously enjoys coaching her from a distance. It helps him to keep in touch with the office and any new regulations which come into force in his absence. He is sent a weekly newssheet by the Inland Revenue and it seems he is still regarded as being on their payroll because of it being a 'reserved occupation'. The RAF pay is more just a top-up from his normal salary. Back in Blackpool things were not brilliant. By March he writes:

> "Unfortunately I have had a dreadful cold on top of the last. I had nearly got rid of the other one when we came down to South Shore and would you believe it, I started with another. I went into a chemist's shop and paid 2d for a draught which they said would help – then I went to the marvellous Woolworth's cafeteria here and got some hot soup and a hot meat pie and gravy for 5d (6d to civilians) - this was to augment my dinner, as we never get enough here, and what we get is

Blackpool, February 1941

75% starch. We have mostly bread, potatoes, butter beans and rice pudding which is the greater part of the day's meals – there is a joke going round that we shall all go stiff with the starch! During Sat afternoon I went to bed for nearly 3 hours and my cold felt heaps better afterwards. I stayed in on Sat night and was in bed early. Then on Sunday morning we were all fetched out of bed at 7.30 breakfast at 8.00 a.m.! - at the last billet we used to stay in bed until 9 a.m.

Yesterday we started in earnest at 7.45 am on the front. We marched, drilled, did PT etc. and then went on the pier – they are using the concert hall for lectures - and there we had an hour's lecture on the service respirator and gas in general – but we do not get a service respirator until we leave here. We were also told to tell all our civilian friends to carry their respirators everywhere at all times – the RAF take a very serious view of gas and we dare not be seen without a gas mask. We also went to the baths, but it was a washout (that's supposed to be a joke) . We squeezed and pushed under hot water showers like a lot of cattle or a sheep dip parade. I was never more horrified in all my life at such a display of human figures and cannot get over this feeling we are just so many 'cattle'!

Last night I went to St Annes to see the Oxburghs. I stayed from about 7.30 – 10.00p.m. and sat in a lovely easy chair in front of a nice fire. You will appreciate this point when I come to a description of the billet.

Most of today we have drilled, PT'd and marched and had lectures on the pier. One on gas and the civilian respirator, the second by a medical officer on certain diseases, which I found quite

Blackpool, February 1941

revolting and really I do get my eyes opened here! I wish I didn't in a way, as I feel just a bit frightened of life and want to come back to the nest at Louth under Mummy Lanc's wing. Still, I suppose one must grow up and face up to different aspects of life bravely. Then we had a talk by a padre, who explained his position in the RAF as a friend to all, and said we were all in a team and must get the team spirit and must learn discipline of the body in our drill and discipline of our minds in our thoughts. I did enjoy listening to him after the previous lecture, and it sort of restored my confidence in myself. Then he wished us all good luck and said "God bless you" - he was only a very young man too. He told us where we could find him and hoped we would go and see him. He told us to go to the parish church on South Shore, which is called Holy Trinity! I went on Sunday evening and was later invited to a concert in the church hall which was free. It was very nice and there was a great attempt to make you feel at home and it was a successful attempt I think. They sang songs about Spring and being young, my mind wandered to Haugham and its beauty, and the times we spent there. Then there were songs about partings etc. and I think most of us in that room felt a bit moist around the eyes. Fortunately some good community singing followed and that was great fun!

Tonight I ache all over with exercise, particularly around the shoulders – I think it must be pulling my shoulders out which is a good thing. My feet too are burning and are rather sore. Now a word about the billet if you are not fed up with all the letter. Never have I met such miserable people! They have an apparatus for heating water and

Blackpool, February 1941

there are hot and cold water taps in the bedrooms. But they only run it until 6.45 a.m. - we are all called at 6.30 a.m. and if you are not washed by 6.45 you have cold water for the rest of the day. At Blooms we had hot water all day and could wash our feet and could even wash handkies, but here you hardly have time to wash yourself.

Then again last Friday and Saturday we were stone cold and there was no fire – when it was lit, they put on dusty coal which burns for hours, but emits no heat and we are not allowed to have a poker. We all sit round this smoky fire on hard bentwood chairs and get pins and needles! Anyhow we complained and were told if we wanted a decent fire, we must buy our own coal! This comes to 2d per head per week and tonight we are feeling really warm. It was terrible to come in cold off parade where we were kept standing around and then see the fire, but now it is not so bad. For breakfast or tea there is bread, but we buy our own jam as we are so hungry and must get the bread down somehow. These people get approx £22 per week for all of us and I guess they are putting away £12 - £15 of it! They are always peeping in the room and putting off lights if it is not too dark, although sometimes it is dark enough at breakfast and tea. If we ask for more bread and milk, there is such a glare and they look at you shiftily too! Still, we have a better billet than some fellows and it is clean and the food wholesome, although starchy, so I must not grumble too much. Tomorrow I'm going over to my auntie's at St Anne's for tea. Jean has asked me to go to their social club at the church for table tennis and badminton which should be rather fun.

On Thursday I have arranged to go with

Clifford (Eileen's cousin) to see Richard Tauber in 'Land of Smiles' He is going to sing 'You are my heart's delight' and I am looking forward to it, although I do not usually like a lot of singing. I am particularly wanting to see him. Can you come please? I wish you could!

Now I must close as I have all my button cleaning to do and it is 9.00 p.m. This seems such a long letter – not too long I hope - but it has been like having a chat to you and I have enjoyed writing. Goodbye little pal. Chin up and keep smiling and wrinkling your nose. Give my love to Mr and Mrs Lanc and let them have all the news please.

Yours very very sincerely David

PS Sirens are just sounding – for 3rd time since I arrived. Hope nothing happens and I hope you are safe tonight also.

In response to all this Eileen remains fairly sanguine and puts things into perspective. She comments on the bathing arrangements " which certainly sound pretty crude, and I can just imagine your impression, but things like that always happen when there is a huge body of people to deal with; you still have your individual character remember, which as you make friends, will show itself to them and you wouldn't be led in thoughts and ways by other men, therefore you cannot call yourself a sheep exactly." She is herself becoming more inured to the air raids which she calls 'Moaning Minnie'. "There is an air raid on and we are all sitting up, we are getting used to Moaning Minnie, she has played her tune absolutely every night this week, nothing has

Blackpool, February 1941

happened, touch wood, the planes keep passing over. I do hope everyone is OK in L'pool after the Wed night raid; suppose you would hear it." Eileen's grandmother and various aunts lived in Liverpool and she was used to going there for holidays, so naturally she would be thinking of them as well as David. But she is too tired to keep worrying and by midnight decides to go to bed and risk whatever raid is going on above her head. She signs off cheerily. "I remember my little prayer every night, so I'm sure you will get on all right in your new life. Goodbye Sausage. Eileen." The arrival of some photos plus her sensible letter seem to have the desired effect in raising David's spirits. By mid-March he reports:

> "I must tell you how supremely happy I am today. I feel full of energy and health, as the fresh air is doing me a lot of good. I had a lovely time with mother - I've got an excellent billet – and I feel you are so dear to me and rejoice in the knowledge that you are my friend. This last reason makes me most happy and I put my heart into my work properly all day and began to enjoy it. We are working very hard now, and start at 8.00 a.m. until 12.30 p.m. with about 20 mins break. This morning it was rifle drill i.e. shoulder arms, present arms etc. and learning to be master of the rifle and not let it master you. This afternoon we began at 1.45 p.m. with foot drill, marching, about turn etc., saluting, followed by ¾ hr physical training and finishing at 5.15 p.m. It is much the same most days and is very tiring. Last night I was going to write to you but could hardly keep awake, but tonight I'm not too bad. The continuous exercise makes the arms ache and feet

Blackpool, February 1941

sore and the rifles we are slinging about weigh 10lbs, but at the end of the day my face burns and is red - I feel brimming over with health, although tired and golly! What an appetite I have. At present we are learning to do all the funny things with a rifle which the guards do outside the office.

You will see I have changed my billet and I am now very comfortable. The lady at the last place got a septic foot and could not look after us, so we all got moved. Victor, Ted and I are all in the same place. Vic and I share a room on the top floor and although rather rough, with the type of bed you get on a station, we are very happy – there is warmth, an atmosphere of freedom and plenty of good food. The landladies (2) are charming and say "The boys come first – we come next" and are extremely good to all 20 of us. Mother came in here and met the ladies. She was very pleased and they said to me afterwards they were ever so glad to meet her.

I went with Cliff to hear Tauber and it was wonderful. He sang 'You are my heart's delight' several times and brought the house down. Later the same evening the warning went and planes were roaring about and some guns about 200yds away went off – they did frighten me, but as they were in action on Fri night also I am getting used to them. They made mother jump though! Yesterday we all went into the gas chamber with our civilian respirators to gain confidence in them.

We were then told to take them off and as it was tear gas, our eyes began streaming. This was done to prove to us that respirators are 100% perfect. Are you carrying yours by the way? Please do just to please me.

This week we are on Crowd and Cordon

Blackpool, February 1941

> Control. If any bombs are dropped here, or the guns go off we have to be ready in billet, with overcoats on and gas capes strapped on – so that when we are called for, we are ready to go out and manage crowds, help to clear debris and get people out etc. This is really intended when there is a blitz, which we pray will not come. It means getting up during the night, though, so I hope it does not occur during this particular week. Keep smiling and God keep you safe, dear friend. Sincerely yours David."

Confidence and pride seem to be growing slightly, as is evidenced by his next letter:

> "My Dear Pal,
> Will you come for a walk on the prom with me? I have just spent nearly 2 hours cleaning buttons, 2 pairs boots, stitching on buttons and strengthening others and finished by giving my uniform a good brushing and feel very smart now. The sun is shining gloriously and the sea is very blue. All I need now is a little pal to talk to on the walk – especially if she is wearing her blue costume and the pink jumper – but as I cannot talk to her, I will write instead."

He has by now located the TocH rest room and found a way of phoning Eileen twice a week, so things are looking up.

> "Tomorrow night we all go on guard for 24 hours – we do 2 hours on and 4 hours off until 6.00 pm Tuesday and during the day we have to keep our eyes skinned for officers, as we have to salute

Blackpool, February 1941

them. For ranks below Squadron leader we slope arms (i.e. have it in the left shoulder) and then bring the right hand over the butt as he passes. For ranks of squadron leader or above we have to slope arms, and then as he passes we present arms – rather a difficult thing - then we order arms - send up with the rifle at your side. I am sure I shall stick the bayonet through myself presenting arms! At night we have to challenge everyone we hear "Halt, who goes there?" and stand with the rifle pointed at the person ready to charge. We have also to shout out as fiercely as possible. Then we say "Advance and be recognized." It is pretty cold and lonely at night, but I shall wear your scarf and will pass the time thinking about you all. During the 4 hours off we have to remain in the guard room and if lucky, you get some sleep, but they say the place is very draughty.

Last Fri we went to the miniature rifle range for the RAF, where we practised shooting at a 25yd target, lying on our tummies. Firstly we fired 5 shots 'grouping'. This means you fire the first shot and wherever it went the next 4 shots had to be grouped around the first one. Then we fired 10 shots 'application' – which means each one must be aimed at the bull's eye. I had never previously fired a rifle and needless to say, I waited till someone else fired to see how loud the bang was! It was not very loud, though. Our targets were then examined and a mark given to us. I got 40 out of a maximum of 75 and was told I had passed. Victor got 20. Next week we go on the big range, 200yds, and fire a Lee-Enfield rifle, which goes off with a terrific bang and the rifle is supposed to kick.

Goodbye little girl – keep smiling, the war will

Blackpool, February 1941

> soon be over and life will be great fun for all of us then.
>
> With best wishes David."

Little did he know that he would still be on RAF bases for 6 more years.

Back in Louth Eileen and Mrs Lanc are also getting themselves ship-shape in health. She writes: "The two of us are on parade at 7.40 a.m. every morning. We wear bathing costumes and swim suits and jump out of bed with a spring instead of lying low as long as possible; we then fling the window wide open and do all the Daily Dozen exercises to the wireless. We are stiff all over and walk about with bent backs, so we have sympathy with you now." Although she is trying to apply herself to new tasks at the office, it seems her mind is elsewhere some of the time. She sends a letter to the wrong address and when it is returned, the tax inspector in charge of the office writes "Dreamin' of thee" on the outside of the envelope before putting it on Eileen's desk. Day dreaming is actually what seems to get them through the war. They live partly in a parallel universe, doing what they have to do, but all the time partly elsewhere in their thoughts. It makes long boring days bearable and reduces anxiety when times are more stressful. Many hours are spent communicating by letter which seems to lift them out of their situation and because the postal service was so good, answers to questions and thoughts could be exchanged very easily. Nor were they just writing to one another. It seems that many evenings were taken up with corresponding with various relatives

Blackpool, February 1941

so that most of the time everyone knew roughly what was happening in peoples' lives. In some ways they were even better informed than we are today, despite emails and social media. This is because they were willing to talk about feelings and impressions, not just report facts and activities. It is what makes the correspondence personal and interesting.

Eileen is not sure she really wants to hear about the rifles and David then draws back a little on the detail, in case it upsets her. But generally, they do share their thoughts and worries and it is this which builds the relationship at a distance. Ordinary domestic details give an insight into what their lives consisted of. David's time at Blackpool seemed to be drawing to a close, but he was unclear about when and where he would be going next. He undergoes more inoculations and takes it upon himself to wash all his underwear in a washbasin, in case he is suddenly posted. Again he has a flu-like reaction, perspiring and shivering half the night. They get all packed up to leave, only to find it is a false alarm. Eventually, though, he writes:

> "We are going tomorrow and have received rations and 1/6d subsistence which means a journey of 150-200 miles. How I hope and pray it will be Lincolnshire! I will write as soon as I get there. And endeavour to ring up 223 on Fri night, usual time. Don't count on it or wait too long, as I may not be able to get to a phone. Sorry to be in such a hurry. Your pal David."

He feels at this stage that he is not quite the same

Blackpool, February 1941

person as he was before: "Eileen will compare this photo with the big one and it is very different. I am thinner and mother told me so too. As for the lines and mischievous sparkle, I am afraid life here is rather serious and sobering and the only time one gets a really good hearty laugh is at the theatre or at a joke on the wireless. When I come over to Louth I shall feel carefree, which I'm afraid I never do now and to hold both your hands – and perhaps rub noses in that same old way will make my eyes sparkle, I'm sure. Eileen, I can't write any more tonight. I am so full of memories, such happy ones, I feel I could burst into tears without much effort. Goodnight sweetheart until the morning." Blackpool has been a revelation to him and he is not sure what is coming next.

3
Southend on Sea, April 1941

This melancholy mood was in danger of persisting as he arrived at Southend on Sea because of his mind continuing to inhabit two parallel worlds. He writes:

> Dearest Eileen,
> Lunch hour again and in 10 mins time you will be collecting your bag, pen, and putting on your pixie cap and cycling off to No 1 - to find Mrs Lanc stirring the gravy and just finishing serving the dinner. You lucky girl, I wish I was with you doing the same. I am now in the canteen, having had my dinner. I feel much happier now - last night I posted your letters and went along to the village church. It was so peaceful and quiet and I sat in there about 20 mins before anyone arrived, thinking about you all and where you would be, until my eyes felt moist – you know, Eileen, I am not a very brave sort of chap really, am I?

Southend on Sea, April 1941

It was a nice service with a small choir and pump organ and very few in the congregation. The address was: Do not lose heart or despair and as I listened, I felt it sort of applied to me and resolved that I should not despair. Then I returned to the billet, cleaned up my buttons and was in bed by 9.00p.m. - so I had my little pact earlier.

Today I have settled myself more and rather enjoyed it. We were up at 6.30 am and were transported down to the drome by 7.00 on 'mushroom picking' i.e. wandering over the field looking for craters, time bombs etc, which have to be reported. This was over by 7.30 a.m. so we went to breakfast. We get a cereal and warm milk every morning and two rounds of bread and butter (thickly cut) and cocoa, coffee or tea. The drink varies on different days. With the bread we had 2 sausages and also some lovely jam. After breakfast Victor and I went to the washrooms, got washed, did teeth and hair etc, because we had no time beforehand – then we returned to the billet for parade at 9.45 am. If you are lucky, you can get a lift on a lorry, but otherwise you have to walk the 2 miles. This mushroom picking occurs once every three or four days, so when we are not on it, it will not be necessary to be down for breakfast at the drome much before 7.45 a.m.

During the morning we dashed around in a lorry to 'stores' about 3 miles away and collected overalls, rubber gumboots, shovels and so on and then Victor and I were picked out to go with a corporal filling sandbags. The rest went digging a ditch, so I think we got the best of it. It reminded me of the day we filled them at the office – after I had been to Gainsborough - and I can remember calling you Miss Holland! Our corporal was a quiet

Southend on Sea, April 1941

fellow and we didn't hurry, but stopped every now and then to watch fighter patrols circling around and after filling about 40 bags we went for dinner at 12.00 noon until 1.30 p.m. We had swedes and potatoes and some sort of stewed meat and gravy, followed by prunes and custard.

6.30 p.m. Very soon you will be putting on the pixie cap once more. How does time fly! Do you remember how we used to grope our way home on those blackout nights? It would be lovely to have you so close now, Pud. This afternoon we have continued to fill sandbags – until 4.00 p.m. when we went to tea and arrived home about 4.30 p.m. on the RAF bus. Since then I have been messing about making a fire go without using sticks and we have no grate. I have also made my bed up – the usual wire mattress cum 4 blankets and 2 sheets. This afternoon they asked us for details of our civilian jobs - several fellows said 'clerk', so I said 'Civil Servant, Inland Revenue' which seems to carry more weight – and I saw this written down. This makes me feel more hopeful and tonight I feel remarkably cheerful – the fire is going nicely and we have scrounged two bulbs from stores so the darkness in the house is no more - we have also got stove going down below which heats up the water – and we have discovered a bathroom with 6 washbasins in and also 2 baths. Things aren't so bad now and I am not worrying at all. It is good to feel you are doing some good towards the war even if it is only sandbagging and this station is described as a 'forward station' and is said to be fairly active when unwelcome visitors fly over. It is rather thrilling to be on a station which last September would be one of the most important and perhaps had a say in the bag

Southend on Sea, April 1941

> of 185 that September day. Even if we are Works and Buildings and sort of responsible for station maintenance, we are keeping the wheels going, so I shall put my heart into this job while I have it to do. (I expect you can see a difference in this letter and the last, can't you? I was silly, wasn't I?)
>
> One thing I feel is that I am doing a lot of physical exercise, but no mental exercise – so I shall look forward to receiving your income tax tests and also Mrs Lanc's German, as I must keep my brain active. This type of life will make it rusty. Must close now. I want this to catch the post at 7.00p.m. Cheerio Eileen."

David was an avid student of German and he took to teaching Mrs Lancaster German in the evenings and once in the RAF, he continued to send her some letters in German and to correct some of the letters she sent him. He obviously therefore had mixed feelings about the war itself, although he could see the necessity for it, given Hitler's actions.

Eileen tries hard to boost him up from a distance, joking that with his big feet he is unlikely to slip down a time bomb hole, but she can understand his sensitivity. She hopes he will soon get a job where he can prove his worth and she cajoles him along by saying "And you are a brave chap, at the way you have made up your mind to stick to your principles in spite of all the other fellows, how you have made the best of your new life although it is often very tough; it's only because you think a lot more deeply than most of the boys that you feel rather sad sometimes, hard-heartedness isn't bravery, is it? She herself is becoming increasingly busy at the office,

Southend on Sea, April 1941

routinely being required to do 8 hours overtime, taking on War Damage assessment work and even working on Good Friday. But at least she is always able to go home for visits and it seems to be these that sustain her. Not to mention the milk chocolate which she is sent for Easter! The only thing she seems to be indignant about is the fact that she has now got to start paying Income Tax herself, because she earned £111-10 shillings annually and the exemption limit was £110!!

It seems as if the Inland Revenue very much kept in touch with employees who had joined up and it was customary for employees to announce themselves in the district to which they were posted. Thus it was that David ended up visiting the Southend Tax office and making it one of his social outlets. He writes "I was invited to go down tomorrow evening at 7.0 p.m. to table tennis and another young chap who has registered as a Conchie (conscientious objector) asked me to his house on Sat evening. He is about 27 and is married. It was a most successful visit and I enjoyed being there, talking about the work and the effect of the war on their office. I also had an afternoon cup of tea just like old times."

Mental stimulus appears at this stage to be important for both of them. Eileen takes to writing a few letters in French and she starts wondering whether her job as a Clerical Assistant is actually leading anywhere. Much of her time is spent on either filing or taking letters to the post and it is clearly not stretching her sufficiently. She decides to raise her concerns with the tax inspector, Mr Riordan.

But he preempts her by saying one Saturday morning,

Southend on Sea, April 1941

when they were clearing up the week's work "I have been wondering how I can get you off the filing job." Eileen recounts the conversation. "I then told him that I wanted to be learning something and that filing did not get one very far and he agreed, saying it was responsible work, but didn't carry much glory. He said he wants me to have one of the Half Yearly books next half year – there will be two or three assessment books. I told him I didn't mind staying on filing during the rush as long as I could get more interesting work soon. Then he said that he didn't see why I shouldn't get into the Clerical Grade and that I have been recommended for clerical work. Isn't it marvellous? I know you will be thrilled, because so much of it is due to you. You also told me not to worry and everything would turn out all right and now it seems to be doing so." Her great complaint was the lack of training available in the war, because all the senior staff were too busy to spare the time and the younger men had gone off into the Forces.

David manages to find mental stimulus in a different direction. He is asked to help run some French classes at Southend one evening per week and seems to have enjoyed the challenge. This, in addition to correcting Eileen's income tax tests plus writing copious letters keeps him occupied most evenings. He much prefers to settle down in a quiet spot to read or study. He writes: "Lots of fellows seem to live for the present – having what in their opinion is a good time – but I look forward all day to the evening when I can write as I am doing now." Nonetheless, he hopes he will be put on more interesting work during the day which would either train him in a skill or make him use his brain more.

Southend on Sea, April 1941

Eileen, David and Mrs Lanc

Southend on Sea, April 1941

Up to now there has been no direct contact between them and by April David muses on the possibility of Eileen visiting him sometime when he is home in Barnsley on leave. His parents had already suggested it, but nothing had happened. He writes "My father wrote, saying they were disappointed you could not come and was also rather sorry that consultations and discussions should be necessary, because he said it makes it appear that they are anxious for you to come, whereas the invitation is purely sent to you as a friend, together with Mr and Mrs Lancaster, because of their deep desire to make my leave as pleasant as possible. There is no question of throwing us together, but the fact that renewed discussions are taking place does make it look as though they might be trying to, when in fact they are not."

The whole issue seems to have become quite delicate and eventually Eileen has to explain that much as she would like to go for a weekend "the whole root of the matter is that Mummy and Daddy don't want me to be forward like so many modern girls are and just rush off to Barnsley at the slightest opportunity. Perhaps it would be better to think about it a little longer and also perhaps it can be discussed if the families do meet for the picnic. We are all anxious to do the right thing, so I do hope you will see our point of view. Goodness knows why there are these silly conventions, because our friendship is so marvellous that I'm sure there is no need for all this restriction from the outside world." When one considers that both of them were 20 yrs old by this point, it just goes to show how times have changed in terms of social mores.

Southend on Sea, April 1941

How, then, were they to have any direct contact with one another? The answer lay in the good old public telephone. Trying to ring a box at an appointed time was by no means straightforward. There was no direct dialling and all trunk calls had to go through an operator. People could be kept waiting in cold telephone kiosks for hours in an attempt to get through and once a connection had been made, the system was to push Button A, at which point the money inserted dropped down and was gone. Distance dictated the cost, so some calls were 1 shilling 4 pence, whereas others were 2 shillings 8 pence. One night, when David was worried about Eileen because of a serious raid on the Humber region, he tried to phone at the appointed time. The number he rang went through to a call box and a nearby shop simultaneously. The P.O. shop owner "went up in the air about calls coming to them. I don't know why he couldn't get you to go his phone, as he said he had seen you waiting in the box – I hung on for 6 mins for 2/6d, but he was most unobliging and sounded so annoyed. I am so disappointed and did want a chat with you, dear friend – we have been so unlucky this week, haven't we? The moral seems to be that in future I will ring you at the office on Louth 90." By this time Eileen had started doing fire watching on certain nights of the week and so this became the most reliable way of phoning up in future. If a connection failed and money had been committed, it was somehow possible to lodge a claim with the Post Office for it to be refunded, but it was all a bit cumbersome. The course of true love never did run smooth!

The life at Southend on Sea was a strange one.

Southend on Sea, April 1941

Sometimes David had duties in the cookhouse and at other times he was roadmaking. It was not all hard graft, as he recounts:

> "On Sunday after posting your letter we went over to the road making job, but did nothing except lie down and sunbathe. After tea I set off for a walk, found a nice spot and read Taxes magazines, then as it grew cooler I continued my walk and arrived at the WVS canteen in time for the news at 9.0 p.m.
>
> At 9.20 I decided to play a game of chess with another fellow and Les, the new friend, returned to billet."

Suddenly the leisurely tone of his letter changes and he writes:

> "At 9.25 an exciting incident occurred, of which I will sometime tell you more. It only lasted one minute, but 3 Messerschmitts were shot down round-about – one of which blew up on the aerodrome itself. Les said he threw himself on the ground and machine gun bullets spattered on the wall above his head - but for an insignificant game of chess which never got started, we should have all been together and perhaps have got in one another's way and not dispersed quickly enough. It is a good job that you wrote on the same afternoon 'Keep your fingers crossed for good luck' - I certainly had it. The Works Flight at last proved its worth – we were transported down to the drome at about 10 p.m. at 60 mph singing all the while – and worked till midnight. We returned to bed and then returned at 3.00 a.m.,

Southend on Sea, April 1941

commenced work and worked right through until 1.30 p.m. on Monday with half an hour for breakfast. Golly, we were tired! And did we work with a will and a good heart! By lunchtime one would never know any 'incident' had occurred. Included in our work was the collecting of the many small pieces of Messerschmitt and its pilot and I am afraid it was very gruesome. I pulled myself together and managed to carry out what I had to do, fortunately. Further details of this part would not interest you dear, so let's forget it. After dinner we were given the remainder of the day off and we all returned to bed, very tired. I got up about 5.0 p.m. had a bath and had tea at the WVS about 6.0p.m., then I started your letter, so now I have caught myself up and will close. Cheerio and keep smiling. With love David."

He has been in the Forces for about 10 weeks by now and this is the first real encounter with death. It must have made him think.

4
28 April 1941

At last Eileen and David manage to meet up. It is the occasion of a picnic in Louth which his parents also arranged to come down for as a surprise. Organised by Mrs Lanc, they all go to Hubbard's Hills which is a nearby beauty spot. It sounds to have been a success all round, judging by their letters. David is much more sure of his feelings now and writes:

> "During the last 10 weeks away from Louth I have sometimes wondered: do I really like Eileen as much as I think I do or is it my imagination and the result of always being together? I can honestly say that wavering has been dispelled and that I am most sincere in what I say – we had a lovely time and have added more happy memories to our overflowing store – and memories count for so much nowadays, don't they? The little bridge at Hubbards Hills, with the sun shining and casting 2 shadows into the clear water – the glow of firelight – and the approaching beauty of Haugham – a

28 April 1941

> place which to me is almost 'holy' – I cannot think of a better word. You have helped me such a lot, you dear, and uplifted my spirits to face whatever comes. My mind is far away from my monotonous work and life and this afternoon, when everyone was pretty fed up, one fellow suddenly turned on me and said "What are you looking so pleased about?" I could not tell him I was far away, but my face must have betrayed me! I hope too I have helped you, dear, in some small way – for that is what I always want to do – to impart that same courage and brave spirit to you, which you give to me. To help you to endure and smile as I am resolved to do, until all this is over and we can be together more often in happier circumstances."

For her part Eileen writes: "My dear Old Pal, yes you are my Old Pal again now; it was grand to find you just the same and still as full of fun as ever: all my little doubts about you being different have completely gone now; really Mrs Lanc was sweet to give us such a lovely time. I hope the memory of it will keep us happy and cheerful and help us to smile through whatever distasteful work we have to do in the future."

Yes, they were both essentially the same, but in the intervening weeks each had grown up a bit more and widened their mental horizons. They felt more confident of getting through the war together, even though they would spend most of it apart.

In a wartime situation it seems life can alternate between something very demanding or serious and something very easy and lighthearted. The day of the Messerschmitts had obviously been an anxious one, but in the next letter David paints a different picture altogether:

28 April 1941

"You remember I told you we were doing a different job? Well, yesterday we arrived on the scene of operations, no-one was there and no-one in charge, so we sat about, played football etc until about 11.0 a.m. and then a sergeant arrived and started off about football teams and cup ties and we did about 20 mins' work before it was dinner time. The same thing happened in the afternoon and we packed up at 4.15 p.m - after a most 'strenuous' day. I cleaned all up, had a bath, and then we had a feast – as gleeful as schoolboys in a dormitory – we had got 6 pieces of bread from the dining hall, as plain bread is easy enough to get – but we got butter enough for it also! I was chief toaster and we had a lump of cheese – I can't say where it came from at all – and Ted and I had each got some cakes and Vic had chocolate to finish off with."

Eileen too is always on the lookout for some lighter moments outside of office hours. She seems to manage to go to plenty of dances, concerts and films in between doing overtime and fire-watching. Outings to Mablethorpe and Skegness are still possible from time to time and she thoroughly enjoys her work with the Brownies. At Easter time she puts on a 'Spitfire Follies' concert/entertainment together with her sister and 2 friends. They manage to raise £2-10 shillings which presumably would go towards the funding of Spitfire planes. Again, simple childish pleasures offer a bit of light relief when she is at home that weekend – she recounts finding a smooth stretch of road to go roller skating on and collecting primroses in the woods. Back in Louth the tennis club is getting going again and is up to 34

28 April 1941

members, so the summer looks promising from that point of view.

Organising leave now becomes the predominant activity. A decision has been made that men can have a weekend off every five weeks, which also involves getting a pass to travel further afield. Some men found they could not get to where they wanted to be within a 48 hour period and so they were prepared to sell their turn of leave to someone else. David was seriously considering purchasing some leave for 5 shillings. Sometimes restrictions were put on how far away men could go geographically and round about this time David suddenly found he was not to be allowed more than 5 miles from camp. He was extremely disappointed, having set his sights on travelling to visit Mrs Lanc in Limpsfield, Surrey, where she was staying with her mother for a few days. The danger would be that he could get picked up by the Service Police on going through a London railway station, and "I should be very lucky to get past them without a pass." The penalty for going AWOL would be that he would be put on detention and given extra duties for several days, so it was not worth it. He also could not see how it would be possible to visit Louth either "as it means leaving here 3.45pm on Fri night and passes are not issued from the guard room until about 5 p.m. under any circumstances." Somehow he manages a flying visit to Barnsley arriving there at 9.15 p.m. on a Friday night and leaving at 1.15 p.m. on Sunday. "it was a full carriage, packed with smoking soldiers who found it necessary to swear every alternate word to emphasise their point." He has still

28 April 1941

got his heart set on Eileen joining him when he is next home on a 7 day leave "The last thing my father said as my train left was 'Persuade Eileen to come, even if it is only for the sake of blasting her conventions'!! - blasting being used in the correct sense of the word." And so he travels in hope.

Back at camp in mid-May he gets involved not just in road building, but also in camouflaging various items. It has to be said that David was not a very practical person when it came to using his hands. He recounts: "I am doing some camouflaging with black paint and a broom and have got the stuff all over my overalls and hands. Never have I felt so filthy on a Sunday of all days. We camouflaged the 'thing' so well this morning that one of our Spitfires in landing came straight towards it and only just climbed up in time. We all threw ourselves flat and it passed at about 4 or 5 feet above our heads. It was an exciting interlude, as you can guess."

Outside of the camp he keeps his contact going with the Southend Tax Office and its table tennis club which he visits on a Friday night. Presumably he went in uniform and was regarded as the airman because he writes:

> "The whole crowd made me very welcome. At 9.0 p.m. we had supper in the Inspector's room and it was very daintily laid out - we had macaroni cheese, chocolate blancmange, coffee and biscuits – all prepared by the two girls. When I was leaving, they all stood at the door and crossed table tennis bats, forming an archway for my ceremonial exit!"

28 April 1941

At least this must have boosted his morale, even if back at camp he was not the most practical person. He gets to know a Tax Officer, aged about 27, who is a Conc. Obj.

> "I discovered he was the leader of a Baptist church, so I suppose that is why. He and his wife were very nice to me and we had plenty to talk about - he said I must go as often as I can to see them and if ever I want to have a quiet room for study, I must go there. You know, Eileen, I am beginning to enjoy myself down here now that I have found friends who are so pleasant and of similar views and interests – don't you think I am very lucky? 6.0 p.m. Sunday, this afternoon 2 of us were on the painting job. We finished it by 2.30 and lay sunbathing until 4.0p.m - which is what I like! Have no more news now, so goodnight dear and keep smiling. Sincerely yours David."

It seems as if David has opted to do some studies on bookkeeping in his spare time and needs somewhere quiet where he can concentrate. He has also been asked to teach some of the men German and so will have to spend a bit of time preparing lessons. Eileen is pleased that he will be using some of his mental faculties. "You won't feel half so lonely now that you have something to puzzle about while you are heaving planks and building roads" she writes. She even suggests he ought to apply for a commission in the RAF, but this proves impossible because he has not got a 'Highers' qualification.

She for her part is hoping to sit a tax office exam to see if she can be regraded from an assistant to an officer

28 April 1941

grade, but it sounds as if the exam has been cancelled for the time being. The tax inspector at Louth says she ought to press for clerical work in order to gain valuable experience. "He said there is great opportunity now, with offices being so short staffed and having much more work to do in addition and provided I took full advantage of it by proving that I could do the work I ought to stand a good chance of promotion." She is eager to know how the clerical assistants at Southend tax office managed to get a 'trial on clerical duties' and she wonders whether it is because they are older employees. Wartime often forces people to develop skills or move into new areas of work and so it may have been that the boundaries between assistants and officers were beginning to break down. If so, Eileen wanted to take advantage of the situation and better herself, whilst she had the chance.

Whitsun had nearly arrived and the spring was in full flow. Eileen writes "On Sunday morning Mrs Lanc and I cycled out to Haugham woods, it was a hectic ride, my back mudguard was loose and kept clanging all the way. However, we arrived intact and it was really lovely out there. All the bluebells are out now and it looks a picture. We went in at the usual place and made our way round the chalk pit and eventually came out by the 'broken down straw thing' and the bottle is still there! I pushed it under a little further and there it will stay until July, I hope". Quite what this was all about is unclear, but it seems Eileen and David had had some rendezvous in this place the previous year and that maybe some illicit drink had been consumed. Hence the bottle had been hidden? We

28 April 1941

shall never know, but it is a tantalising thought that these teetotallers had perhaps tried something stronger when just the two of them were together! David teases her in his next letter, but his comments do not really elucidate much. "You must have enjoyed going to Haugham and going to the 'broken down straw thing'. I wonder how it got broken? Some careless person must have put his or her foot through it. People are so inconsiderate aren't they? And to leave a bottle around is very untidy. It will be moved in July, won't it? (or even in June, you never know)." It is obviously some in-joke between the two of them, but quite what is unclear. They might be mildly amused and embarrassed to think I have uncovered some secret 78 years later!!

Whitsun Bank Holiday Monday for David was to be spent at Oxted with Mr and Mrs Lanc. He had managed to negotiate a 48 hour pass and was looking forward to a complete break. A little after that he becomes a bit more adventurous and decides on the spur of the moment to hitch down to visit one of his mother's family friends in Merton Park. He writes excitedly: "I felt in the mood for a thrill last night, so I hitched to London from Southend. I rode in the back of a van from Southend to Chadwell Heath which was as far as the driver was going — a distance of about 30 miles. I stopped the next passing car which took me through Ilford to Forest Gate. Still on the main road I stopped the first vehicle which was a big 6 ton lorry, going to Westminster. The driver was a chatty fellow and as we went along through the East End, over Tower bridge and on the Old Kent Road, he gave me a running commentary on where I was and I saw the most

28 April 1941

dreadful bombing. He dropped me off at the Oval Tube Station and I took a 7d ride to Morden, my destination. I arrived here an hour before I should have done by train, although I only left Southend 10 mins before the train had! And I saved about 2/6d!! It was very thrilling and satisfied my lust for adventure." This was presumably the first time he had been able to witness the devastation of the Blitz in London and it must have made quite a deep impression on him. In the days of no TV, we forget what an impact such a sight must have had. He arranges to visit again the following week, but this time a return trip up the Thames is planned to go as far as Windsor, which apparently will last 12 hours. He is beginning to spread his wings and gain in confidence.

Eileen meanwhile is enjoying the outdoor life, attending an open air dance at the end of garden fete at the Nurses Home "it was jolly hard work dancing on the grass, but we had some fun, careering round the rhodedendron bushes etc." Becoming rather skittish in her letter, she signs off with a drawing of what looks like a steaming Xmas pudding, presumably because her nickname was Pud. Then she adds, in brackets, "Illustration is not a new type of Nachttopf" (i.e.potty). The warm weather must have been loosening them up a bit and both were enjoying a bit more freedom in the light evenings with no blackout.

The prospect of a joint visit to Barnsley is now becoming more real, as apparently parental permission has been granted for something to happen in late June. There is mounting excitement on the part of both of them and David wonders whether Eileen can perhaps

28 April 1941

persuade her boss to let her return on Tuesday so that then "we should perhaps get a day on the moors." For some reason he has been put on peeling potatoes all day in the camp "until my hands are ingrained with dirt and I can hardly hold my pen", but he is also pleased to report that an Intelligence Officer has sent for him and given him some German leaflets to translate. So he seems to have an odd mixture of tasks and is not sure where any of this is leading. There are rumours of 30 Works Flight being posted to Egypt, but these come to nothing, so it is hard to predict what will happen next. Hence the Barnsley leave is the only definite and the main goal to be achieved in the short term. Life in the Forces, he concludes, does not necessarily hold the glamour one might suppose, looking on from outside. He writes: "I was marching round Rochford, boiling hot, clothes sticking to me, NCOs growling 'Swing those arms' – with us were Home Guard, Army, AFS and ARP personnel - and a band- I remember when I was little and would wave a flag and think it wonderful to be marching with them - but I was glad to be out of it, I assure you - that place where I can be with you in spirit, if not in person."

Barnsley came up to expectations for both of them and they managed to visit Hugsett woods in the time available, but not the moors, as Eileen could not spare the Tuesday as leave. The Civil Service had reduced leave to one week per annum because of the war and as she pointed out, she was lucky to be able to return to the office late on the Monday morning as a special dispensation without it cutting into her annual entitlement. It

28 April 1941

The visit to Barnsley. (*Left to right*)
Back row: Mr Lanc, Eileen, Mary Laws aged 17, David (aged 21), Mrs Lanc.
Front row: Mr Laws, Helena Laws (aged 11), Mrs Laws

seems she had quite a sympathetic boss who allowed her to make up time later on, but whole days were not negotiable. Terms of endearment in the letters now seem to be changing over time, as the relationship develops. When she writes in French, she has moved from 'vous' to 'tu' and instead of 'My dear David', she puts ' My dear Laddie'. He for his part addresses her as ' My sweet little sister' or 'My sweet friend'. They write frequently every few days and he plans a trip to Louth 3 weeks after the Barnsley weekend.

Eileen settles back down to office life, which is punctuated by running a Brownie rally and taking her

28 April 1941

mother to Sutton on Sea. They managed a picnic on a grassy slope, but as she commented "One isn't allowed to go on the seafront at all at Sutton, but it was lovely to breathe the sea air and we got quite sunburnt." The east coast was barricaded off as a form of defence and this must have seemed very strange to them, as they had always gone to Sutton on Sea for their carefree summer holidays in the past.

The office is stretching her more with new work and plenty of variety "I'm primarily on claims and help with Half Yearly too and today Mr Riordan has given me some Schedule E as well. I'm to assess the schoolteachers and Policemen. I know you will be pleased to hear about this Laddie." One has to remember that at this stage, there was no PAYE system and everyone had to be assessed individually. The country needed tax for the war effort and so in a way it was an important job to make sure revenue was properly assessed and collected. The tax office was essentially quite a serious place with mainly older employees who had been there for years. But there was occasionally a lighter side to the proceedings. Eileen writes: "Old George was trying to demonstrate how good he was at climbing the greasy pole and he clambered up the sides of Mr Bowder's steel press and the whole thing fell right over, he crashed onto the floor and all the contents of the cupboard shot out. Mr Bowder gave a start because he thought it was bombs and he looked most unamused and annoyed to see his orderly books and papers scattered about." One of the men, called Polk, seems to have been a younger chap who used to croon at lunchtime, singing popular

28 April 1941

songs whilst pretending to hold a microphone to his lips or improvising with the cord of the light pulley. Such were the simple amusements of little Louth tax office.

David, back at base following the Barnsley trip is now very caught between all his memories and the demands of the present situation. His father has written approvingly of Eileen which is a great encouragement to him. "We think Eileen is a very nice girl – a charming girl – and such a contrast to the type these modern times produce – a type which I loathe." David is trying to improve in his shooting accuracy "The range is a little clearing surrounded by lovely trees and paths and we had a wonderful lie in the sun until it was our turn. I have not heard the result yet, but the consolation is that my ears were not affected as badly as the time we fired at Blackpool – it made them sing and hurt a bit, but not as much. But for my ears I should enjoy the shooting you know, but it just takes the fun out of it when it hurts." Nowadays they possibly would issue ear defenders and do risk assessments, but not in the wartime years. David had had a mastoid operation when he was a child and it had left him with permanent damage to the eardrum. It was just as well he had not become a wireless operator and had been classified as a 'medical reject', even though the term sounded a bit harsh.

The weather must have been quite hot in the summer of 1941 because Eileen recounts swimming in the canal, climbing over the lock gates and standing in a waterfall the other side of the gates. The war is perhaps having the effect of making her more adventurous generally and when she is home for a weekend she dons a bathing

28 April 1941

costume, wanders about the fields and splashes about in the brook at the bottom of the garden with her brother, Norman (now aged 14). She hopes to be able to take David to the sea when he next visits. David envies those who can just splash about and swim in rivers. "People were swimming in the Thames yesterday" he writes, but because of his ears, he always had to be extremely careful where water was concerned. The trip down river to Windsor seems to have made a great impression on him and he muses "It is most beautiful and there are some lovely shady willows every so often, where boats were moored and some lucky chap with his little pal sat enjoying the peace and serenity of it all – calm water, hardly flowing, bees and dragonflies about on a warm day and Nature, Nature everywhere. We two could sit for hours and never tire of it. Perhaps not talking, but silently enjoying it all, holding hands perhaps – Oh my dear little pal – it would be so lovely!" Impractical and cack-handed as ever, David spoils this idyllic scene by recounting how he nearly lost the oars, "the boat wobbled dreadfully - then a steamer just missed us – finally we got settled down and everything was OK."

The planned weekend in Louth draws closer, but it seems to take a lot of organising. There is the need for an early pass from the sergeant who is resistant to letting men go off site because it is War Weapons week. Then there are ration cards to be negotiated which last only for the 48 hours spent away from base. Trains are not that plentiful and David anticipates leaving camp at 1.30 p.m., but not arriving in Louth until 10.08 pm. He finishes his letter by saying "Mrs Lanc is a dear to

28 April 1941

have me and put up with me – I hope I don't seriously encroach upon her rations." Mrs Lanc was resourceful and this must have stayed with her for the rest of her life, because I remember visiting her in 1972 and she cooked a simple sausage casserole by slitting the sausages lengthways and eking it out with plenty of veg. She was a homemaker and she was unfailingly generous hearted. David often describes himself 'cochonish' (piglike) in letters, but I doubt that he would overstep the mark when staying with people he admired so much.

The contrast between enjoyable weekends and boring weeks seems to be becoming more evident over time. David admits "My main concern is to get on the least distasteful job, where I can keep clean. I am shocked to find myself volunteering for church parade as an alternative to work – for it is a dreadful service and I prefer to go to Rochford church anyway - because I'm afraid this is the wrong spirit to go to church isn't it? I'm afraid the majority go unwillingly when they are detailed for it and the whole system seems wrong to me."

The next weekend what he sets his mind to achieving is to go to Limpsfield where Mrs Lanc's mother has a cottage. He is becoming a bit cavalier, announcing that "I shall have to come by train if I get a pass and by various ways if I don't. It will be too bad if I am stopped going and I shan't care if I am caught coming back." He is aware of the dangers of travelling without authorisation and says "I shall have to be careful, as it is Bank Holiday, and there has been a lot in the paper about forbidding troops in London over the weekend. There may be extra

28 April 1941

police about. It is most likely that I shall hike to Redhill and there is an hourly bus service from there to Oxted." It seems he got away with it.

The contrast of sunny summer days and sad experiences all intermingled comes across in some of his letters. "Yesterday I was part of a funeral escort and it was most depressing on such a glorious day – but I got over it. I hope I don't get sent on any more. It was the funeral of a bomber pilot who, returning from a sweep, crashed onto our field. It was bad enough watching the crash - I was only 400 yards away – never mind having to attend the poor chap's funeral. The burial was about 12 miles from here at Benfleet, so we got quite a trip out of it - I disliked being present anyway - as it makes one think too much - just when one begins to forget that there is any danger. Still, we all whistled and sang on the way back and the mood of depression cleared from everyone and we felt quite gay by the time we had got back and had dinner – it's all in a day's work and is just another job, I suppose."

It seems that whether working or resting, days in camp can appear rather strange and meaningless. David recounts time off at Southend in the following terms:

> "I decided not to go to Mrs Parkin's, as I was so tired. Instead I lay on the bed reading this month's Taxes until I fell asleep and awoke about 9.0 p.m. I popped down for supper and then turned and slept until 9.0 a.m. Tues morning - I went to a little cafe in the village and had toast and coffee for breakfast, in the garden under an apple tree – leisurely reading my paper. I stayed here until about 11.0 a.m. then returned, swept up the room and

28 April 1941

also an electric light bulb which I had knocked off the holder with a sweeping movement of the hand whilst putting on my shirt!! By then it was time for dinner and afterwards I went into another cafe just outside the camp and listened to the news. Then I returned to the billet finished off reading 'Old Pybus', had a bath, an early tea and went down to Southend with Les to the pictures. We got out about 8.0 p.m. and went along the front towards Westcliff. It was a glorious sunny evening and the Kent coast was very clear the other side of the water. We wended our way back and found an obscure little Salvation Army canteen in a back street – two old ladies were serving the food and there were 2 soldiers in there. On the walls were posters such as 'Welcome', 'Do you pray?' 'Write that letter to mother now' etc. the type of thing which I think tends to drive away the ordinary tommy rather than attract him there. It reminded me of what Fred Crosby said when we first opened Toc H. 'We mustn't have too many parsons and dog collars about the place – it will frighten the lads away'. Then we hitched back to Rochford as all the buses were full and would not stop and it was about 10.30 p.m. by the time I was in bed."

It sounds like a rather aimless existence, trying to fill time as best one could.

There is quite a lot of disorganised or empty time, it would seem. For example, he is detailed to attend a dental appointment 30 mls away in Hornchurch, but when he arrives, no-one knew he was coming "So back we came in time for tea, having had an afternoon's joy ride!"

Periodically the reality of war does break through,

28 April 1941

as he explains: "Today I saw a Wellington and a Stirling bomber which had been to Germany last night and had to land on the way back.

A Wellington is a big thing and you could put a Spitfire under its wing – but my goodness! You can put a Wellington, as huge as it is, under the wing of a Stirling. They are tremendous things and I have never seen such a big thing before."

On the whole though, life is mundane. It comes down to potato peeling usually, but as the war progresses, David finds more streamlined ways of getting through the task - "we have been on spuds for the last 2 days. We started by scraping them and then brushing them with scrubbing brushes as they were new potatoes. The latter idea was excellent, but we developed it still further by putting potatoes in a bath tub with an inch or two of water and scrubbed them with a stiff broom, changing the water about 3 times. In about 7 minutes we could do a stone of potatoes and got finished in no time." I wonder if David, who usually liked things to be clean, actually ate any of the potatoes himself?

He is generally frustrated by his work and decides to put in for re-mustering. He thinks, on balance, he would be better suited to radio/wireless mechanic and puts in an application to this effect. Meanwhile, he has to fall in with general expectations of Works Flight 30. He describes as follows:

> "This week I have been combing the drome and I feel like a walking multiple store – wearing gum boots and carrying my ordinary boots as the grass is so wet, together with gas mask and tin hat, a rifle

28 April 1941

and a bandolier of 50 rounds of ammunition. We have entered the 'invasion period'. In fact we sleep with the confounded thing by the bed and also a Tommy gun and 1000 rounds in the bedroom. Added to all this I may also be carrying a rain cape! This 'invasion period' is quite a nuisance. On Thursday afternoon the relay gave out the notice 'Practice, practice, practice only. Man all aerodrome defences'. We put on tin hats and gas capes and I was apparently in a stretcher party and went running round the trenches with another bloke, carrying a stretcher. We couldn't get any customers, so we sat down and waited until the war was over. It was most realistic and waves of planes came in from the sea. The worst about these stand-to exercises is that they may come at any time, without notice. This morning we had further Tommy gun lectures, and one of our sergeants was lecturing and with the magazine loaded, was demonstrating. He was fiddling about with it when it went off with a terrific bang and 3 neat holes appeared in the hangar roof!

It was a good thing it was pointing upwards and not at us grouped around him. He was certainly very careless and was lucky to get away with it – you are never supposed to lecture with the gun loaded."

It sounds remarkably like an episode of the TV serial 'Dad's Army'. David carries on his letter in a completely different vein and says

"At last we have got our second caps and tunics, so when I come to Louth. I shall have a brand-new cap and tunic and my best pants are almost new, as

28 April 1941

> I haven't worn them much. I shall have to come in uniform, unfortunately, in order to get cheaper travel, but anyway it will look smart to be seen with the little lass.
>
> I heard a rumour that I may do the clerk's work in the office this weekend, as he is on leave. It mainly consists of answering the phone, making out work reports and translating into English the Warrant Officer's dictation and any odd job. Little did I think when I started a new office job at Louth that I should be beginning another type of office work down here 4 yrs later."

In fact he would have been far more suited to it than all the rifle practice and roadbuilding.

He starts to become reflective about his lack of RAF career, comparing himself with a man they both knew from Louth, called John Musgrave. He had become a pilot.

> "John has been very successful and is to be admired. How wonderful to have achieved an object and feel satisfied.
>
> It makes me feel so disheartened and rather a washout when I think of wings and a commission – what I would give to be in his shoes! And whilst thinking about this I have been weeding and sweeping all day. You have certainly set me considering once again about applying for a commission. It would be on the administrative side though and the more I think about it, the more it appeals to me. I have put in a re-mustering form for clerk, special duties, about 3 months ago, but have heard nothing about it. I would do

28 April 1941

> anything to get away from this uncongenial work and surroundings."

He begins to realise though, that things could be worse. Three of his friends Vic, Les and Ted, are suddenly sent away for an indefinite period to a new station near Cambridge.

"They took shovels with them, so it looks like work. The camp is a very isolated one, miles from anywhere and I am glad I haven't gone. I was down to go, but the WO said I had my French and German classes to keep on and that saved me." These classes were quite a source of extra income at 7 shillings per hour. Also, if he had gone to Cambridge, he would have lost his 7 days of promised leave.

He later hears news of his pals "they are in an unearthly place called Hunsdon nr. Ware. They have to wear gumboots all day long as it is a new camp and inches deep in mud. They are 5 mls from a railway station and 4 miles from a village, pub or cinema. There are about 100 cottages nr the aerodrome and there is a weekly dance. Sanitary arrangements are not at all pleasant."

Little does he know that he is about to get posted there himself, after all.

5
Hunsdon Nr Ware, 3 September 1941

"You will see by the address that I have moved. I arrived at Rochford about 10 p.m to find Acacia house full of Canadian soldiers. I slept on the aerodrome last night in the reception hut and travelled up here this morning. I arrived about 3.0p.m. - we are about 27 miles from London. All I can say is Southend was heaven compared to this – it is very rough here and it is going to be hard going. I shall be able to read and write plenty, I think, which is what I like, and I shall be living for your letters dearest. It is so awful here, I am seeing the officer immediately about my commission or remustering. I had no luck with the phone call tonight – delay on the line of about 2 hours. Goodnight darling – but for having you to think about, I could literally weep about this place."

Ever practical and encouraging, Eileen tells him

Hunsdon Nr Ware, 3 September 1941

to "keep your chin high, though" and comes up with various suggestions for social contact in the area. "There is a man in Hertford Tax Office whose name is Mr Hull and who is the head in charge of the YMCA movement there: he apparently was a friend of Mr Crawley and is a very nice fellow. The other person is a Mr Jackson who is the caretaker of the Priory at Ware." Presumably this is the way in which introductions were made before the days of Facebook and internet, but it was important to have some links, especially in a new environment.

Eileen, for her part, is having a better time of it and she writes "I came home yesterday ... and Mummy and I are going on the spree to Matlock tomorrow." She admits:

> "I suppose on the surface the war hasn't affected my life a great deal in comparison, but you know I sometimes think how lovely it used to be when I was first in Louth and I had no overtime to do at the office; and how we two used to go bike rides, walks and to the flicks and so on; the war has robbed us of all these things and some days I have felt rather disheartened; but now I've decided that it's foolish to let conditions - which only last for such a small proportion of one's life - influence me too much; besides our friendship is so marvellous that it buoys us up and helps to lift us out of our present life."

Their youth was passing by, David was to turn 21 the following week after going to Hunsdon and he must have wondered where his adult life was going. Eileen was more optimistic. She writes on returning from her holiday "As usual, there was the normal accumulation of

Hunsdon Nr Ware, 3 September 1941

work awaiting; still I'm not bothered, I expect the war will be over before I've dealt with the huge pile of war damage correspondence."

So what was Hunsdon really like? He writes

> "The camp is a big one, perhaps 3 times bigger than Southend. Our Works Flight is in a T-shaped hut and Ted, Vic, Les and I have got our beds together. There is plenty of noise and din, card playing etc until about 11.0 p.m. so that if you want to turn in early, it is difficult to get to sleep. Lights out is at 10.15 but there is a certain amount of laxity allowed. I miss the peace of the room we had at Rochford and am denied an escape even at night from the unpleasant, but it must be endured. The hut is not properly finished off and water drips in when it rains – and one's underclothes always feel damp early in the morning. Near the hut is an ablutions hut, with bowls, mirrors and 4 baths, but never very warm water. I have had two cold baths in two days, but as the weather gets colder, the water may get warmer. Next to the ablutions is the most disgusting 'duck egg' (toilet) I have ever seen and that is as much as I can discreetly say.
>
> The cookhouse and dining hall are a large country manor in beautiful gardens and it is about ¾ mile away, right off the camp, as are also the offices – pay, accounts etc. Thus, we walk about 4 miles a day for meals and they are not really worth going for - the food is not so good and not very plentiful and Southend was a palace compared to this. Plates are not particularly clean and the tables are dirty. I am afraid we all suffer from hunger and this is not alleviated by canteens, as there is only one canteen, the NAAFI. There are no WVS canteens or anything in Hunsdon or St. Margaret's.

Hunsdon Nr Ware, 3 September 1941

Dad

Hunsdon Nr Ware, 3 September 1941

Mum

Hunsdon Nr Ware, 3 September 1941

> In the NAAFI it is a question of queueing and to spend 6d about all you can get is 6 cups of tea! They have no chocs or cigs and the place is built to accommodate 350, whereas there are 1800 here – the Southend NAAFI was three times the size.
>
> At Hertford I understand there are some good canteens and cinemas and there is an RAF bus every evening at 6.45 returning at 10 - 4s.8d return, so I shall be going over there often, I hope. It is very decent of Crawley to offer me some addresses and I shall be very pleased to have somewhere to go, only I do hope people won't think I am too pushing or sponging.
>
> The work we are doing here is mainly spade and digging. We are split up into parties and Ted is in charge of us. Les and I are with him and one or two of the nicer fellows – none of my 'tormentors' are in our party."

By the next time he writes, he reports "as regards the wetting of the bed by the dripping of the trees overhanging the 'ole in the 'ut – I have manoevred my bed so that the dripping drips on either side of the aforesaid bed" and he takes Eileen's and Mutti's advice to spread his cape over the blankets.

David is clearly struggling, so he thinks he will seek out the padre for advice and put across what his interests and skills are in the hope of being moved sideways. There is also a new officer who is overheard talking to the WO "he said I want to see all the more intelligent men in the Flight – who's this schoolmaster Laws and who is Salmon? I want to interview them and form some sort of educational classes, so that these men can interpret official instructions to the others in their own language."

Hunsdon Nr Ware, 3 September 1941

But it sounds as if there are more basic immediate problems to deal with. He writes:

> "There was no water in the tank on the site, so Les and I set off across 2 ploughed fields to a farm pump, dragging 2 cases of water in the dark. By the time we had done all our chores it was time to start getting supper ready. I had a tin of oxtail soup which we mixed with water and boiled in our mess tins. Then we had Oxo and cheese and bread and butter."

Eventually he does get to see the padre who agrees he is in the wrong job and who promises to see the Adjutant. David seems to feel guilty that he is not contributing as much as he could to the war effort.

> "It makes me really envious to see the pilots here, young lads of 19/20 flying Hurricanes – and I wish it could be me. I seem to have lost all that fear I had before I was in the RAF about flying and would love to be among them and achieve some sort of ambition. They seem such a nice crowd of fellows, these sergeant pilots and I have been working around their quarters recently and have heard them talking together. Then, with a sigh, I realise such is not my luck and bring back my thoughts to the work I must do – the ignorance I must put up with and endure, my discontentment, the rough hut instead of the decent quarters. Still, I am trying all the time and yesterday's interview may be the turning point."

It is hard to disentangle how much of David's attitudes were a reaction to mixing with a different

Hunsdon Nr Ware, 3 September 1941

class of person or how much he really would have been able to cope with flying a plane in a war situation. I tend to feel he would have been out of his depth facing such an immense level of risk, although obviously he would have enjoyed the camaraderie of the other men. What he really seems to be baulking at is the tedium of his RAF existence and his generally subordinate position.

> "Today has been rather tedious – drill and a ranting sergeant, whose morning bacon must have been burnt – and then further restrictions and attempts to make life more of a concentration camp. We are now to march to meals instead of leisurely strolling down reading the paper or talking. We have also got to get our breakfast between 7.0 and 7.20 or not at all - previously we had it when we liked, provided we were on parade by 8.0 a.m. There is also talk of allowing us out of camp one night in four, but this has not yet materialised."

He is beginning to appreciate what he had before Hunsdon "Last night I wrote a letter to the ladies of the Rochford canteen, thanking them for all they did for us – one is made to realise how much we depended on them now we are away from there."

Much of camp life is following standard routines e.g. "Friday night is cleaning night. I donned my overalls, got down on the floor and scrubbed around my bed space with a brush and cold water. Then Victor had a cloth and wiped over and between us we had soon done our 2 spaces. It was funny to see everyone scrubbing, cleaning windows, dusting etc. and there were lots of

Hunsdon Nr Ware, 3 September 1941

jokes about charwomen, 'a woman's work is never done', housemaid's knee and Friday night is All-Bran sorry! Amami night. (I get these adverts all mixed up)."

There is also routine testing of equipment e.g.

> "yesterday we all went through a gas chamber to test our respirators. I have been through one twice before with a civilian respirator, with tear gas, but this time it was D.M. gas – a nose and lung irritant which they consider is likely to be used. My respirator is quite effective and we wore them for 2 minutes. Then we took them off for a minute and breathed the gas. It was quite pleasant and had no immediate effect. After we had been in the fresh air for about 3 minutes, we started coughing, one's nose and throat irritated and it just felt like bronchitis. It also made you feel sick and very depressed. We were told the main point about the gas is its delayed action and if you breathe some and then put your mask on you begin coughing and get a suffocated feeling inside your mask and are apt to lose confidence in your mask and take it off in desperation for more air, when of course you are finally gassed. You have to endure it and keep the mask on until the coughing goes. To really experience it gives you great confidence in your respirator and you lose all fear of a gas raid if there is ever one. I wanted to tell you this as a good bit of advice, so don't be frightened by my description will you, little lass? Tell Mutti too, won't you?"

The routine of billet life and behaviour was also fairly predictable each week e.g. "Last night was a very rowdy one. Half the fellows in our hut went to a dance and a

Hunsdon Nr Ware, 3 September 1941

booze-up. Vic, Les and I were in bed when they all rolled in about midnight in various stages of drunkenness and very merry. You never heard such a din! They were tipping one another out of bed, throwing pillows and biscuits (i.e. mattresses) about, shouting and singing for about ¾ hr. It was impossible to sleep through it."

What effect does the whole thing have on other people who are not used to life in the Forces? It is hard to know, but a snippet in one of David's letters is interesting. He says: "Another fellow in our mob, who was never very bright, seems to have taken a turn for the worse and has now started playing trains – buying imaginary tickets at imaginary booking offices, giving up his place to imaginary ladies – I think it is the first sign of the cracking (mentally) of the Works Flight!" Perhaps resorting to obsessional behaviour was a means of coping for some people.

For David the answer was to engineer pockets of peace and quiet away from the noise. He manages to find a WVS lady who is willing to let him and Ted rent a warm kitchen where they can study in the evening for a minimal charge of 2 shillings a week. He reports excitedly: "There are also easy chairs and electric light. It is next to the NAAFI canteen, so I shall be able to slip out for buns and cakes etc. for supper." The chance to concentrate is highly prized. He has by now set his sights on studying via a correspondence course for the Senior Tax Officer qualifying exam and so sends for various Instruction Books from the Inland Revenue Association. He is apparently advised that he can omit the Preliminary tuition course and go straight for the Advanced course.

Hunsdon Nr Ware, 3 September 1941

In this way he feels he will be achieving something at least, which could later pay off in civvy street, even if his RAF career amounts to nothing.

As the colder weather begins to take hold, the search for warmth is in their minds. Even when doing the road building they make a fire "There are 4 of us on our particular job including Ted and myself, and we make a fire each morning so that we don't get cold when we – ahem!- stand about. After scrounging wood, paper etc and getting it going it is about 9.15 a.m. and at 10.15 our lorry arrives to take us to the NAAFI for break. We are back on the job by 10.50 or so and finally pack up for dinner at 12.15 and parade again at 1.45p.m. This afternoon the fire was so nice, we roasted some chestnuts and finally went to tea about 4.45p.m." It sounds a bit like the great British workman.

Perhaps the First World War song "Keep the home fires burning" is an indication of how much servicemen longed for the comfort of a fireside when they were out in all weathers and dangers. Certainly warmth and a welcome into someone's home is always very much appreciated and commented upon by David in his various letters. "Tonight I am in St. Margaret's – Les met some friends at the chapel and they told him to call and bring a friend, so here we are, spending Sunday night in a comfy room with 2 very sweet elderly ladies. People are so very good to us, aren't they? We have been chatting and are now sitting down, writing letters."

Fortunately, after all the leaking huts, the men are moved to some senior NCO's huts, which are very comfortable. "Rooms 8ft by 24 foot and four in a room.

Hunsdon Nr Ware, 3 September 1941

We have a little stove and heat our water and do our cooking at supper time. There are shelves, pegs and as we are at the corner of the hut, we have 3 windows. The floors are lino instead of wooden boards. We couldn't be more comfortable. The only discomforts are the mud and the lack of a proper water supply. We fill a can up at night and have to use it very sparingly."

All is going fairly well by this stage and a weekend's leave is scheduled, when suddenly plans have to change, as a 'mock invasion' is planned. No-one is to be allowed out of camp and David has to send a telegram, saying he is not coming after all. In a follow up letter he writes:

> "these mock invasions are a nuisance, but are inevitable and there is nothing I can do about it. We wander around in gun capes, helmets and all the rest. Some of our lads are to be prisoners and some guards for prisoners. There are to be bombing attacks etc and manning trenches, but I have got a fairly good job. The Intelligence Officer sent for me, and as he knows no German, I am to accompany him when he interviews prisoners. In each prisoner's pocket is to be a slip of paper in German, giving details of his unit etc. My job is to translate these slips of paper for him. He is going to lend me a book of German army and air force terms tomorrow to swot up. That is the only bit of fun I shall get out of the weekend – when I ought to be going to such a nice dance with such a nice little girl."

The actual exercise turned out differently from what he had expected. David said it was a 'farce'.

Hunsdon Nr Ware, 3 September 1941

"Sat 8.0 – 12.30 p.m. sat around in the office waiting for Intelligence officers and prisoners. Nothing happened. Wearing capes and tin hats, of course. 1.30 p.m. - 4.30 p.m. Alert given – standing around again, imagining what I ought to be doing in Louth and thinking about Blue Eyes. 6.0pm. - 9.0p.m. Attack alarm given. Slipped out of camp by unofficially knowing the password "Nuts" – and slipped back, having got one blanket from the hut. 9.0 p.m.- midnight. Lay down on floor of an old hut with everyone else – one blanket between Vic and self and cuddled up for warmth. It started to rain very heavily and dripped down our necks and on our feet – we got 2 hours sleep in before this, however.

Midnight. Had a mug of stew which had been fetched from field kitchen –Vic and I changed to a drier spot. 12.30 a.m. Rain came in – went back to old spot and got 2 others to move up and squashed in. From then on until 3.0 a.m. never slept a wink as so boiling hot and stiff from hard floor – fellow behind snoring down my neck – Ugh! 3.0 a.m. Got up and stretched legs etc for a while, then saw someone using 3 blankets - carefully removed one without wakening him, and went to sleep alone with blanket and overcoat. 3.30 - 4.30 am – slept, but very cold – all awakened at 4.30. Detailed to walk over to field kitchen and help carry breakfast rations. No plates etc just hands and a knife and bully beef and bread. 6.0a.m. The alert continued – sat around in hut just wasting time until about 7.30-7.45. Went on guard with 5 others - rifle, bayonet, freezing cold until 10.45 a.m. Three dreadful hours - felt very sorry for myself. Did imaginary shooting at armoured cars, tanks, and dive-bombing aircraft. Thought lots about Blue

Hunsdon Nr Ware, 3 September 1941

> Eyes and what Sunday would have been like with her. 11.0 a.m. Guard changed – thawed out and had some dinner - invasion over about 2.0 p.m. All sent out roadmaking, as usual, and were made to work hard until 5.0p.m. 6.0p.m. BED – you bet - to dream of what next weekend will be like!
>
> The weekend, which should have been one of the very best, actually was the hardest and most miserable one I had ever had, but I don't feel too bad now. I can laugh when I think about it."

Periodically he does manage to escape the camp for a weekend in Louth, but returning by train in the time available does not always work out and once he gets stuck in London, having missed the last train. "The YMCA at Liverpool St was full – all beds taken - but by a bit of luck I met one of our fellows who had also missed his last train and together we got permission to go onto the train which was waiting till 4.25 a.m. We lay down on the seats covered by overcoats and I wrapped my pyjamas round my head and laid it on my gas mask. I could have done with your scarf, dear. Despite all this it was very cold, but I slept till about 4.0 a.m. The walk was even colder and we arrived in camp about 6.45 am - my pass was OK at the guard room so everything is alright."

He copes with Hunsdon life by living in his imagination and hanging on to good memories and this leads to some of his letters becoming almost lyrical. Round about this time he writes:

> "This morning I saw two beautiful scenes and as I watched, I felt 'I must tell Eileen and share this with her'. I went to Holy Communion with Victor and

Hunsdon Nr Ware, 3 September 1941

it was lovely in the church. Quiet, peaceful and an atmosphere which steadies one's thoughts and aids concentration – I think about you here and manage it better than any other place. Sometimes I think it is God that helps me and that He wants me to think about you and wants to help. The sun came up through the stained-glass windows and a long shaft of sunlight swept across the dark oak of the choir stalls, onto the blue carpet – another beam came through and scattered its light over some Michelmas daisies. Little specks of dust appeared in the light, played with one another and disappeared again. On the altar the golden light reflected from the candles, showered itself over the altar rail and all was bathed in light and peace. It was lovely – a lovely moment and I wanted to have you there very badly then, to hold your hand and share that lovely moment. As I came out of the church, the wind was blowing wildly, scattering the brown leaves around and looking over the fields I saw the sunshine on the distant woods. The trees all swaying, shades of green, gold and brown, a lovely blue sky and fleeting clouds which unkindly hid the sun, but only for a moment. It was at this sight that I felt entirely transported – my mind flashed to many a Sunday morning last year when the wind blew summer away. Where was that little girl in a blue costume, who would have fitted into this lovely picture? The wind would have blown her curls all over, made her cheeks glow and how proud I should be to go and walk beside her. These two beautiful moments have made this day worth living and having shared them with you, I will say goodnight and God bless. Always your own David."

Hunsdon Nr Ware, 3 September 1941

Eileen's letters are more prosaic. She recounts how she got stuck in a toilet at work for more than ¾ hour and had to be rescued by the Inspector of Taxes, who gave the door "three terrific lunges and finally burst it open." She will often tell a joke against herself, probably in an attempt to cheer David up or give him some feeling of connection with his Louth tax office. If she goes to a show, she will relay a few of the jokes or describe a sketch in detail. Her letters often end up on a positive note of "We are keeping our chins high, aren't we" and so she tries to keep his morale up in between visits and phone calls.

The phone does sound to have been quite a difficult means of communication at times. David writes: "I had such a lot of things I wanted to tell you, but the line was bad and here there were boys making a noise outside – and two people waiting to come into the box who, I know, were listening and laughing at all I said." Quite often the call completely fails and then, it seems, he is able to reclaim 1/4d from the Post Office via a longwinded process. He also finds ruses to cheat the system, on occasion, by only putting in half the amount required. "When I ring up Oxted, I have to put a shilling in. Instead I put 6d in and wait a bit. Generally the operator says 'Go ahead please' and I don't put my other 6d in." Eileen would often receive a call in the evening on the nights she was fire-watching in the office.

Although this system worked well on the whole, it meant encroaching on the office territory of the tax inspector. She got a terrific shock one night to find him still in there, doing overtime and so this was quite

Hunsdon Nr Ware, 3 September 1941

a source of embarrassment. Similarly if David rang the office during the day, she could not really divulge her feelings because of all her colleagues listening in to the call. So the conversations became stilted and difficult.

Occasionally an operator would allow a call to be booked a couple of hours in advance or give the person extra time on a trunk call, but this was quite rare. Hence letters always remained the main vehicle for communicating feelings and thoughts.

The best thing, of course, was to meet in person. By the late Autumn of 1941 there is talk of a dance in Louth to which they are both invited. It will be like 'old times' and David makes sure to take his dance shoes. "I have been anticipating it for so long and the exciting moment when my train arrives! Hurrah! I shan't forget my dance shoes either – and I'll bring the moon with me too!" The weekend is a success and consolidates a lot of thoughts.

Afterwards David reflects upon where things have got to by the end of this quite difficult year. "I am glad you think I am enjoying the adventure of the RAF because I am doing – Only in the last few weeks have I realised it. I always feel I can smile, however rough things are – and am really having an excellent change. An open-air, healthy life, plenty of exercise, experience of looking after oneself, finding out the good and bad in the world and weighing them up, meeting all sorts of people, having a fine time on my leaves and days off and especially when I come to see that dear little lass – really it is doing me no end of good, provided I can still remain my old self and keep to all those principles which Mutti and I have set out long ago now. I cannot

Hunsdon Nr Ware, 3 September 1941

say I am unhappy, but shall not be really happy until I am doing better work."

The re-mustering form had got lost in the system, there was some dispute about whether his medical fitness had been correctly recorded and whether he was eligible for clerical work or a radio mechanic's training, but it did seem as if things were moving in the latter direction. He was really hoping for a break from Hunsdon and its routines.

He was also trying to work out what he was like as a person or how others perceived him. Whilst staying one weekend's leave at Merton Park with Mrs Parkin (his mother's friend) they look at a book of horoscopes and he feels validated by the one he reads for himself – "Fertile imagination, keen on study, not ostentatious or pretentious. Fond of a quiet life without show. Conscientious in whatever work you maybe engaged, but rather lacking in push due to insufficient self-confidence or belief in your own abilities. This weakness would be overcome if you make the effort. You will be keen on science and have a great love of nature. You will be quiet and undemonstrative, but capable of making and holding friends of the opposite sex. You are liable to have many changes of place and many journeys." The only bit of this horoscope which he did not agree with was "Beware of marriage until well after middle life"!!

Certainly changes were afoot and he needed to be ready to meet the next set of challenges. "The officer recommended me for my radio course last week. He asked me what I knew about wireless. 'Nothing' said I. 'Did you tinker about with it as a hobby?' 'No' said I.

Hunsdon Nr Ware, 3 September 1941

Then I told him how I could apply for ab initio training with matric and a knowledge of maths and physics. He grew more interested and asked about my civilian job and then said 'I will put your application forward'. I was so pleased and am sure you will be. Little lass come and jump for joy with me the first step is passed."

Eileen, too, has news on the work front

> "At the office we have had a memo down which concerns Clerical assistants and ESTs; it states that there is going to be a review of all of us, a questionnaire is to be sent to the Inspector, he is to send reports of the capabilities etc of everyone who is performing work applicable to the Tax Officer grade. According to the memo, the field for promotion is going to be opened up and the only stipulation is that one must be able to do the work.
>
> Provision has also been made for those who are doing some work above their grade and are not fully capable of taking the position of a T.O. at present, an allowance of 6 shillings per week will be given in these cases and the promise of a further review when more experienced. I think it is really marvellous and I know you will be just as thrilled as I am about it. I am determined to work very hard now that there is at last a goal to aim for. Polk has offered to lend me his Instruction Books whenever I want them, so I have got over that difficulty."

Christmas is fast approaching and this time they have graduated from chocolates as presents to cufflinks and handbags. The only problem being that Eileen has been

Hunsdon Nr Ware, 3 September 1941

unable to obtain the set she wanted to purchase and David (typical man) has forgotten to get on with present buying in time for Christmas. He writes: "Do you mind if your handbag does not arrive until after Xmas, as I shan't have time to get it before? It was silly of me not to think of it in time to get it in Louth last Saturday, but when you're around, I seem to get quite absent minded."

Christmas itself is to be spent apart. He will be in camp and she will probably be travelling with her family to maternal Grandma Hinton in Liverpool. After Christmas he has been invited to join Mr and Mrs Lanc in Limpsfield and a bit later he has leave to go home to Barnsley.

The RAF clearly tried to put on a good feast for the boys and because there was a new cookhouse which had just been built at Hunsdon, it made this possible. Eager anticipation of the festival comes across in his Christmas Eve letter:

> "Tonight has been cleaning night, as usual, and our room looks like a palace. The ledges have been dusted, lamp shades wiped, the floor scrubbed and then polished, all boots and slippers and buttons cleaned, and all photos, Christmas cards, odd articles of clothing etc hidden away in the kitbags. We are very house-proud and strive to be the best room in the hut. (Our trousers are hanging from a peg, but I regret to say there are 'oles in hour trousers pocketses, which still return after being stitched up). On Xmas Eve the sergeant let us have the lorry and we all went down to Hertford. I went to a dance until 11.0 p.m. which I enjoyed very much, but I should have enjoyed it more if

Hunsdon Nr Ware, 3 September 1941

I had had you as my partner. One hasn't got that lost feeling after each dance, when one returns to a chair with a sweet blue-eyed partner, who smiles so sweetly. I slipped out of the dance and rang up home to wish them all the best. Then at 11.0 pm our lorry went back. Some fellows were drunk, some very merry, and I felt intoxicated with the excitement and the spirit of the moment. We sang loudly all the way back to camp and then went round to the rooms of those in bed, and sang to them, shook their beds up and down and generally made a terrific row until about 1.0 a.m. Then we formed little groups and had some supper until it was nearly 2.0 a.m. No-one in our hut awoke until 8.30 a.m. and of course it was too late for breakfast – I was wild because it was bacon and eggs and coffee. However, we got the fire going and had toast and treacle and tea in bed and it was about half past eleven before I was finally up.

The great dinner was at 12.15 p.m. and was in our new cookhouse. This is a fine place, seating about 1200 with big cooking ranges, fish frying ranges, hot plates, plate washing machines and everything is clean and well lighted. Near the new cookhouse is a large new NAAFI canteen and shower baths and wash places. The whole has been under construction for nearly 2 years and must have cost thousands. The tables had tablecloths on them, paper serviettes, mineral waters, rosy apples (I got 3 – cochon!), biscuits and cheese. We all got seated and the officers and sergeants waited on us, brought our food to us and got us second helpings. For the first course we had turkey and pork, mashed potatoes, mashed carrots and turnip, brussel sprouts, stuffing, apple sauce and gravy. Then followed Christmas pud and white sauce,

Hunsdon Nr Ware, 3 September 1941

> of which I had two helpings. Each man's mug was filled with beer and I had a bit of mine, then mixed it with ginger beer to make a sort of shandy. Then we were given 10 cigarettes. There were loud cheers at the end and a collection for the cooks. They got £8 in pennies! After this small snack we all staggered back to our huts and fell asleep on the bed. I woke in time for tea which was lovely boiled ham. Then in the evening another chap and I wandered round the village and into the village hall, which was deserted. We found a radiogram and played records for about 2 hours, just as if we owned the place! I went to bed fairly early and read a book Mr Parkin has lent me *Tomorrow to fresh woods* by Rhys Davies."

All in all it sounds as if the men were given a good time and as if food was in plentiful supply.

For New Year David managed to wangle a short trip to Limpsfield and was no doubt spoilt again with Mrs Lanc's cooking. His final letter of 1941 goes into a reflective mood, contemplating all that the year has brought and wondering what lies ahead. He writes:

> "I had such a lovely day yesterday, with you almost with me, and having you so near but yet so far seems to have made me super happy and yet extra lonely. Last night, with time on my hands I walked through the moonlit city (i.e. London), gathering impressions which I felt I wanted to share with you – it was misty moonlight – quiet and deserted. I glanced at the little spot where we waited for a bus at London Bridge station and then made my way across London bridge itself – how very quiet it was. Great wharves,

Hunsdon Nr Ware, 3 September 1941

warehouses and blasted buildings stretching up to the sky, their huge outlines silhouetted in the light night. Below me was the river, quiet and hardly moving, but looking black and sinister – not a gay Father Thames but one who was scowling, or so it seemed, at the damage and atrocities around him. Looking over the bridge were two young people – gazing as we gaze at our 'rushing waters'. Theirs must have been a heaven, as it is for us, and my heart gave an extra bump with the memory - it does now as I write - do you remember 'Sweet as lilting music, memories return' and then 'Making hearts feel happy, Full of wishes true' I like those words so much you know dear. The signs of war, so close, must have been far away for those two, as they are far away to us when we are happy.

Over the bridge, and the street was darkened by tall massive buildings, large pillars, large entrances and many brass plates on the door. I was entering the city on almost the anniversary of the big fire blitz, and it gave me a thrill to walk there – the only small figure with these huge buildings around me. It was so peaceful that I could not picture the whole place on fire. I crossed over a narrow street which branched off to my left and something loomed up in the bright sky – it honestly made me jump – so suddenly did I come upon it – it was the Monument - erected to the memory of the Great Fire of London and how impressive it looked. At the corner was a policeman and warden and I made sure of my way from them. They were cheery cockneys, very obliging, but I felt I wanted to shake their hands and congratulate them as heroes - to thank them for keeping London still here for me to walk around and enjoy such a grand experience as I had last night. I wended my

Hunsdon Nr Ware, 3 September 1941

way up Cannon Street and Bishopgate and finally reached Liverpool St. I had been slowly walking for about 25 mins, drinking in everything - feeling very receptive for impressions, and just dying to pass them on to you, with whom I like to share everything, joys and worries, happiness and tears, and hope I have succeeded in passing them on.

And so it's New Year's Eve – do you recall last year at this time – I would just about have got back from Barnsley for the dance in the Town Hall. It was a fine dance – with searchlights - and do you remember how we chased round the balcony at midnight, breathless and happy. Gosh, what days! What a momentous year 1941 has been! I have had great changes and uprootings, but seem to have found my feet in life and planted them firmly after shifting about on soft sands. I have come to know you and love you more, little lass, - you played such a big part in planting those wobbly feet, and shaping a sort of unfinished character into the person I feel myself to be today.

And what of 1942? For you I hope it brings much happiness and good health – every success in your work, now that promotion is on the way - and good luck every day. For us both, I am sure it will bring yet a deeper understanding of one another, greater joy in a wonderful friendship, and strength, with God's help, to face up to all difficulties. And for us all perhaps the end of the war. May God keep you safe little lass - I love you so much I should hate anything to happen to you - and a very Happy New Year – keep smiling dear. Most sincerely yours David (Laddie)."

6
From Hunsdon to Leicester, 1942

Eileen has had a good Christmas up in Liverpool with her grandmother and countless aunties and cousins. She has decided that it is not worth having a handbag as a present, as the ones on sale are made of imitation leather, "so I thought I would like a fountain pen with a very fine nib for writing in Assessment books at the office; but if they are very expensive, please don't trouble to get one will you?; the nice Christmas card and letter were what I value most." She is still looking for his cuff-links, but has scoured the Liverpool shops without success. As to the war, she only comments briefly "The bombing in Liverpool is very terrible, but it is useless to talk about it; fortunately near grandma's house has escaped fairly well except for a stray bomb or two. We had no warnings at all during our visit."

Back at Louth, she reverts to all her previous office

From Hunsdon to Leicester, 1942

life and is learning to follow CI Memos on various tax issues. "I've been doing the one about Schedule E and Half Year programmes, deduction schemes and all the Wartime relaxations; I feel like relaxing myself by now." She finds a way of improvising a table tennis table so that she and another girl can play at the office in the evenings and the tone of her letters remains lighthearted. She includes little diversions such as a crossword puzzle and a sketch, taking off David being showered with soot when he tried to clean a chimney in the billet. She is also pleased with her wage rise of 6 shillings.

By the end of January news of his move to a radio course at Leicester has come through and she is genuinely pleased for him. "Oh boy, what marvellous news this is about you really starting on your wireless course at last, I guess you are thrilled to be doing a job that seems worthwhile, after almost a whole year of boredom. It would be grand if you could be billeted with Mutti's cousin in Leicester; really I had to laugh when yet another relation popped up at just a convenient place, I think if they send you to the Arctic Circle, Mutti will know the person who lives at the North Pole."

This did not materialise, but he is accommodated in a civilian billet with a Mr and Mrs Waddington at 39 Evington Street Leicester. He describes them as old age pensioners and says "she is very fussy and looks after me – I had a cup of tea in bed (!) and the food has been good up to now. I am alone here." It would be a change from the noisy billet, but a good opportunity to study properly. The only drawback was its position "Most of the blitz on Leicester was round this part and

From Hunsdon to Leicester, 1942

there are great gaps in Evington Street and surrounding streets and even the house next door but three has been demolished. It is certainly a warm spot!"

The course was being run at Leicester Technical College for a period of 17 weeks, divided into 3 slots with an exam at the end of each. He has to learn how to solder as well as understand the theoretical side of wireless technology. The tuition is divided into shifts "we are going to start the late shift tomorrow – dinner at 12.15 and then work from 2 to 10 p.m. Some days we get the morning free and some days we have to return for games etc. This goes on for about 2 weeks, whilst we are on DC (direct current) course and then we go back to ordinary time on AC (alternating current) course."

Eileen is a bit disappointed that he is not able to get a pass to visit her in the first few weeks, but she pins her hopes on seeing him at home for her 21st birthday which is Feb 14th (Valentine's Day). The issue is how to get from Grantham to Billingborough. She explains that her father, who has a vehicle, could meet her in Sleaford, but "he has two landgirls away, so he is very busy just now and also the petrol is a real problem", so David will have to find his own way through somehow.

There do seem to be buses either from Bourne at 4.20 p.m. or Sleaford at 6.00 p.m., but she is anxious he should not miss too much of the party which starts at 5.00 p.m. Hitching may have to be the answer, she thinks. She has made up all sorts of competitions and games for the party and "it's going to give us great delight to watch you puzzling over them."

The course proves quite demanding and time

From Hunsdon to Leicester, 1942

consuming. "Ever since I came to Leicester I had seemed to be rushing about, no time to think of anything but work, and then finishing late at night I used to drop into bed with a head buzzing with wires, graphs and definitions and never seemed to be able to have one of those real 'little pacts' I found so much time for at camp." The first exam was "not too bad. We had a surprise practical on Wed night and with the instructor standing over you, you get all flummoxed! He gave me 2 dry batteries, one big and one small flashlamp battery and asked which had the greater voltage. I looked all over for some indication (like a chump!) and there wasn't one and stood with the things in my hand dumbly looking at them – then it suddenly occurred to me they were the same! Then I had to arrange resistance wires to form certain effective resistances and also calculate the resistance of an ammeter which had a 2500 ohm carbon resistor in series with it as a multiplier." Sensing that Eileen may by now not be following his account, he interjects "Does this interest you?" and then teases her by saying "I'll be measuring your resistance next time I come to Louth and will bring some wires and meters with me and tie you all up!"

He has made a new friend called Les, who is billetted almost opposite and who is a maths/economics grammar school teacher from Fife. They let their hair down a bit once the exam is over and arrange to take 5 girls to a dance where there is a big cinema organ which plays in between the band. He is full of it afterwards:

> "I do wish you could have come to the really marvellous dance – it is a beautiful hall and it was

From Hunsdon to Leicester, 1942

a very select dance – there were 8 of us in the party and we had a very jolly time. There were all sorts of dances - not too many slow fox trots - there was a statue dance which was very funny, but I will have to demonstrate it to you. There were spot waltzes and a raffle with about 20 prizes. The lighting effects were marvellous and of many colours. Les and I took 4 girls home. We wandered over Victoria Park, that being the most direct way, slipping and singing and laughing. Les is very quiet and shy, but when he gets warmed up, you wouldn't know him! I'm sure we awoke the whole neighbourhood. Then we quietly slunk home about 1.30 a.m. - two airmen who are due in at 11.0 p.m. according to orders."

As expected, the practical side of the course proves more difficult for David than the theory. He had big clumsy hands and was not good with tasks requiring fine motor skills. He is disappointed to find after several weeks that his workshop assessment is low.

"Being brought before the Education Officer meant I must have got less than 50% on the work I had done, and I felt very perturbed because I knew I had done the things almost as good as I could. He told me to see the man in charge of workshops, who assesses us, and on Wed I did so. He said he was surprised I had been picked out and said the figure the Education Officer had must be on the first 2 or 3 exercises and I am now up to Exercise 11. He said I had improved since then and in confidence told me my next workshop assessment which will shortly go before the officer would be 75% and that the work was quite satisfactory for him. We are not supposed to

> know these marks, but knowing mine made me much happier and a little more confident."

Eileen is more dexterous with her fingers and she embarks on a typing course run by Mr Lanc's daughter, Evie. She enjoys learning how to space out headings, type columns of figures, forms of address and attending to general layout. In a neat type written letter to David dated 19th February 1942 she announces "Tomorrow night I am going down to the school to practise. I shall leave the office about a quarter past five and be there until about seven o' clock, then I intend to go to the young people's club which has its first meeting to try to get people interested again. The vicar's wife is going to be the secretary of it this time, so it ought to go much better. How I wish you were here to come too because we're going to have a lot of dancing and the vicar is bringing his Radiogram across, which should be much better to dance to than the old piano."

It seems as if she really enjoyed dancing of all types. By the end of the month she is teaching the Brownies folk dancing; "the kiddies enjoy doing them and try very hard to get the steps right. I've found by giving marks to the best patrols, they take great pains to get them right." At school Eileen had enjoyed some sports (esp. cricket), but was never very good at gymnastics. One of her school reports had said 'Tries hard, but is a little heavy'. It seems as if perhaps her weight was generally against her and she does get teased at the office for this. Her nickname of 'Pud' persists, but she does not seem to mind too much. She tells a joke against herself and recounts "Polk has thought of the bright idea of

From Hunsdon to Leicester, 1942

dropping Joan Brailsford and I over Germany to prove that the rationing isn't affecting us." It certainly sounds as if Eileen is having quite an enjoyable war around this time with plenty of good food, nice activities and more interest in her work.

David goes down with a very bad cold and is taken into sick bay for a few days. He writes: "They looked after me quite well and embarrassed me twice a day by asking me how my 'BARLS' were. Really it's ever so funny, especially when a nurse asks you!" His visit home to Barnsley is delayed as a result, but he tries to go the following week. Meanwhile he becomes embroiled in a misunderstanding with Mutti Lanc. She seems to feel she has been rather neglected by David, probably in terms of lack of letters since he has been so busy on his course. She and Eileen had been ill in bed and she berates him " You hard hearted brute, you didn't even say you were sorry I had been ill." This really quite disturbs him, as he likes and respects her so much. He writes to Eileen for advice on how to handle it:

> "I have had it on my mind for most of the evening − (it's been cropping up among a mass of information about transformers etc every now and then). What makes Mutti think things like this − that I do not consider her, do not think about her? Had it struck you the same way? I don't know why she should say this when I have been chasing the town for her book etc. and since coming out of hospital, have been round 6 or 7 booksellers examining their copies of Shakespeare. After all, I have seen Mutti since I came to Leicester, whereas I haven't been home for 8 weeks, and surely she shouldn't mind if I go home this week

From Hunsdon to Leicester, 1942

> because I was unable to do last week. Tell me, little lass what you think about it. It worries me if I have offended either Mutti or you, when I am far away, as such things are always so difficult to 'settle' by correspondence and often lead to more misunderstandings."

It seems as if they did discuss it and both realised that Mutti was wanting to regard them as her substitute Ersatz children and that there was a tinge of jealousy if they wanted to head back to their respective families. Eileen seems to be cautioning him to be understanding of Mutti's feelings.

Eventually David can see it and writes "it is up to us as her ersatz children to try and drive away her loneliness in life, and just to think a little deeper – that things which might not occur to our own mothers may occur to her. We will do our best, won't we?"

Nonetheless, he does need to get back to Barnsley, if possible. When he does eventually go, he manages to dodge all the Service Police and arrives at 9.15 p.m. on Saturday night. Whilst at home, he sorts out a lot of his tax instruction manuals and arranges for them to be sent to Eileen for safekeeping and for her to benefit from. She is, however, now moving on to some new tax work which he knows nothing about. It was called Post War Credits. People were required to pay additional tax in some circumstances in order to help the war effort, but the idea was it was on an IOU basis. After the war, people would be reimbursed for the extra which they had paid. Many elderly people objected to this, fearing that they would not live long enough to see compensation for their overpayments.

From Hunsdon to Leicester, 1942

Easter comes and goes. There is an enjoyable trip to Billingborough and this time her father has enough petrol to drive David to Grantham for the bus back to Leicester. Again there is the fear of being collared by the Service Police who seem to hang around bus stations. He writes "I hopped out just before the terminus, as a precaution, and posted my pass in the box and returned to bed." The answer is to travel as lightly as possible. He explains that all he has on him is a gas mask, so that on his outward journey "I will hardly be picked out of so many airman in Grantham on a Saturday night." If he had been stopped, apparently the punishment would be to have to report every hour during one's free evenings for about 3 or 4 days and also losing a month's passes.

Time is going quickly and a typing exam is coming up for Eileen plus David is 3 weeks away from his finals. She seems to have quite enjoyed the challenge. "I think there is nothing more satisfying than being tested on a subject which you feel you know something about."

Whilst the typing might be going all right, life on the office counter is not. The case makes the local newspaper as a court case. She writes: "We had a very awkward old chap from Threddlethorpe to deal with, where he was accused of Profanity to a clerk in the Council offices – here he refused to complete his 42/43 return, aired all his grumbles about taxes, red tape, committees and said how the Agricultural Mortgage Committee had thrown him out on the streets, in fact 'I'm as good as a dead man' he said, raising his voice, and those were his words as he went out. I felt like telling him to communicate with Hell, as I should think he will be dealt with there, severely too I hope."

From Hunsdon to Leicester, 1942

It all sounds rather an overreaction when one thinks about how people nowadays often are abusive to official staff, but perhaps it demonstrates the prevailing manners of the time. Amazing to think it turned into a court case.

Although it is springtime, the weather is very cold and the office is not allowed any heating after April 30th. They have exhausted their supply of coke too and are forbidden from ordering any more. Eileen hopes that the boss, who is on fire-watching that night, will experience a frost to make him reverse his decision. This gentle little lass can appear quite hard at times, it seems! Later she reports that the temperature is 49 degrees [F]. "Mr Bowder refused to do fire-watching the other night because of the cold, and he has been reported for neglect of duty."

Back in Leicester David recounts that he is studying by candlelight because his landlady is worried about the gas, which presumably was also rationed.

As the weather warms up, Eileen is looking forward to David's next visit in May and daringly suggests "It would be nice to go to Sempringham Abbey for the morning service wouldn't it? And I shouldn't think it would be too unconventional to have a piggy back on the way home in those rural parts!" Their next rendezvous after that is to be a trip to Limpsfield, once he has got his wireless examination over with.

7
Moving to Bolton, June 1942

His next course is based at College in Bolton "entirely taken over by the RAF. There are about 1600 airmen and it is almost like a miniature station with medical and dental branches, stores, pay accounts, a padre and plenty of officers. Our CO is a Wing Commander. Discipline is very strict, but if one uses a bit of common sense it is easy to keep out of trouble."

It seems he has gone there to learn how to apply his wireless knowledge to working with real planes and equipment. The course is for 14 weeks 8.0 a.m. - 6.0 p.m. every day, including Saturdays. Passes are allowed once a month from 6.0 p.m Sat – 11.0 p.m. Sun and only extend for a maximum of 50/60 miles radius. Eileen starts referring to it as Stalag, however his digs are quite acceptable with a Mrs Mather in Hurst Street. He reports a major event: "For tea today I had tripe

Moving to Bolton, June 1942

and pig's trotters! I wish you could have seen me eating it — trotters are the most difficult things to manoeuvre on one's plate and I don't think I shall have them again!"

Once again David is working out where he fits in the scheme of things. He is impressed by a sermon from a visiting chaplain who "preached on that feeling of 'personal insignificance' — that one doesn't count for much in a large world — in which one is swept away by events out of one's control — and that from this feeling one was inclined to say 'Oh well it doesn't matter what I do or say — or whether I have any standards of right and wrong, as I don't count.' He pointed out how wrong it was to get this idea and how each one of us is continually under God's watchful care — and that we do count quite a lot. He illustrated from several parables and personal anecdotes. Really! He held his audience breathless, I thought."

Unfortunately, two of his mates Les and Issy have been sent to an interim camp at Filey, so David is again looking round for some compatible friends. Initially he is not sure about Eric, a corporal, who seems to be rather full of himself. Interestingly, though, David would meet him again by chance after the war and they became lifelong friends. But during this period there seems to have been an element of competition between them. He is what Les would call a 'blether' — one who is always talking about himself and what wonderful things he has done. "He goes out every night and tells me I am a 'queer sort of cove' staying in or going to the fields. We had a minor argument tonight when I told him my interests were correspondence, German etc. Yet again, I have to be careful with him, as he is a corporal and is in

Moving to Bolton, June 1942

with the NCOs here. On the whole he is quite a strain, but I just let him blether away."

The first 3 weeks constitute "revision of all that they know plus lectures and lab periods on the charging and care of accumulators, using the charging apparatus there will be on a station. All this service equipment seems quite dazing at first, but I suppose daylight will dawn some day. Then we had PT today, although the gym is a big empty room with no equipment. Its not a patch on Leicester's gym."

His landlady sounds to be a homely type and "has taken a liking to them both. She says the last 2 airmen were well to do and made her feel 'reet 'umble' – she used to stand in the scullery eating her dinner as she didn't want them to feel uncomfortable, but 'Yur all reight – Ah could tell as soon as yur cum in' and she doesn't feel 'umble anymore. I thought it nice of her to say so, because I should hate to feel she was not at ease with us." David is generally very impressed with the friendship and hospitality of the Bolton people and it is not long before he is being invited by his landlady's sister, Mrs Cunliffe, to join in church activities and dances. She and her husband also ask him round to their home "You can't imagine what this really means to me – to have these friends, as part of my trouble here has been adjusting myself to a new way of life."

Before the course starts in earnest there is a clothing exchange parade. "I was told off for bringing two frayed collars without having tried to wear them inside out, anyhow I got two new ones and that's all that matters."

The work concentrates on RAF receivers which he describes as 'very neat jobs'. He is issued with a text

Moving to Bolton, June 1942

book *Standard Notes for Wireless Mechanics*. Air Publication 1938. "It is a good book and we have had instructions to keep it confidential etc so it must be fairly important information in it." They progress to learning how to tune a "13 valve superhat – which is so selective you only have to grin at the whole box of tricks and it goes off tune" and then they work on the "Marconi G.P. - commonly called the 'fruit machine'."

After a few weeks he writes:

> "Time passes very quickly at the College now – this week we have got onto much more practical work – with perhaps only one hour's lecture per day. We have been on the receiver R.1082 and transmitter T1083 – these are general aircraft to ground communication sets. We have also been on the Transmitter-Receiver TR9, which is carried by all bombers for intercomm among the crew, and for communication between planes on a flight. Firstly we learnt how to tune these sets and in the TR9 lab, 8 of us working in pairs tune up 4 sets to the same transmitting and receiving frequency, and can speak to each other, by transmitting to the other sets who receive you – then switching over to receive and hearing the reply which they transmit – apart from that each pair is in communication with one another - we each have headphones and a mic.
>
> It is great fun and proves whether your tuning has been successful, as if you are wrongly tuned and start transmitting, the others will not pick you up and you will not be able to receive them – and is just like being in a plane using intercomm or speaking to another plane.
>
> After that we have a look inside and do

Moving to Bolton, June 1942

some circuit tracing - then go into a lab where on these different sets there are deliberate faults, breakdowns etc which we have to locate and get the set working – sometimes the silliest fault - perhaps a small bit of paper in a switch contact, so that nothing happens when switching on!! Another we found was a piece of wire from which the rubber insulation had not been cut off and it was screwed into a contact – the latter gripping the rubber and not the wire! Sometimes there is a more serious fault which takes some finding."

He has got to know a man called Alwyn, aged 21, who was also at Leicester. "We usually work together in the lab - our motto 'The sets I don't bust, he does! He said today how he hoped we got posted together when we leave here." Les also turns up again, so he has a pal from before, which helps.

He also has a number of relatives who live in Lancashire and so makes a point of visiting them from time to time. His cousin Derek is a medical student whose family lives at Heywood and when he visits him, they go long walks in wooded countryside around Rochdale.

It is hard to know what either Eileen or David think about the progress of the war itself. Occasionally they do refer to Churchill's speeches being uplifting and Eileen comments on news or conversations which she overhears. For example one night she is travelling back from Cleethorpes in a train and "we were in a carriage with some Air Force boys and one of them was chatting to me and then he started fervently discussing the mistakes we have made in the Libyan campaign. A Grenadier guard sat in the opposite corner and I could see him writhing when he heard the gist of the conversation, although the Air Force lad was sticking up for the tommies and saying it was a shame that they were always handicapped by lack of suitable equipment and leadership; I didn't agree with all he said, as I found his views rather extreme, but it was interesting to discuss it." Generally, though, they are more taken up with their own everyday concerns and interests.

For Eileen at this time it was a question of organising a Brownie Rally, planning all the games and competitions and going around the shops to find some little articles suitable for prizes. Several of the girls came from a children's home, having been evacuated from Hull, and she was keen to give them some individual attention and treats.

David is getting more and more involved with the wireless receivers "We are now on the Marconi Aircraft receiver - sister to the 'fruit machine' – it is a lovely set, but so complicated. It has 'magic eye' tuning and most intricate direction-finding apparatus on it. It does need some studying and the prospect of probably (!) having to teach it later on makes me shudder." It seems that his corporal instructor has asked whether David would like to be put forward as a probable instructor when he has passed the course and this is giving him a "higher objective to strive for than just a mere wireless mechanic." But he notes "I shall have to work much harder if I intend to get it."

For Eileen's family their main concern at the moment is to have new milking machines installed on the farm at Billingborough. Everything is taking longer than

Moving to Bolton, June 1942

expected - "Pauline, the land girl didn't come in until about 10.30 p.m. as she had been to Grantham pictures with the man who is installing Daddy's new milking machine - romance on the farm; Daddy thinks it would have been cheaper to have had the job done before she arrived, as there would have been no distraction; she does get teased about him."

The war is there, but life must go on. Immediate everyday concerns often win out over international issues. Love seems to preoccupy people more than war.

Although the main work was on radios, the RAF also required airmen to undertake military exercises from time to time. David describes one of these in a rather satirical way:

> "This morning – oh groans! the alarm went off at 5.15 a.m., when all good girls with blue eyes are in bed (and are likely to remain there for another 5 hours) After a fresh morning walk to college we arrived on parade at 6.30 a.m. (still 3 ¾ hrs more for Blue Eyes) and our platoon went in a bus to join the Home Guard platoon. We were split up into a group – about 8 or 9 Home Guards and 6 airmen with rifles where we took up our position by a road block (unfortunately not the one outside No 1). We were well on the outskirts and there were woods and fields around. First we rolled concrete cylindrical blocks in place and then placed the railway lines in 't'oles int' road ' They were just like those cylinders on the hill near St Marys Lane - it always was my ambition to shove one of those. Then we mounted a guard, 2 of us, and stopped everyone for identity cards – pulled up cars, searched buses and had some great fun. As the day

Moving to Bolton, June 1942

> moved on, groups of silly girls continually passed to and fro through the barrier, just to have their cards examined by real live airmen. We were not on the barrier the whole time – I had a position behind a low garden wall watching a road and a hill slope for signs of the enemy, for about $1^1/4$ hrs. I never saw them at all, although an umpire came along and said we were all surrounded – somehow we got all unsurrounded, because our platoon was intact on the outskirts, while the enemy had occupied the Town Hall and most of the town. Word came through that the town was taken and the enemy had turned around and were turning round to mop us up. We left the road block and took up positions in long grass and on hillsides overlooking the place the enemy should arrive – I had a front position where I should see them first and mow them down (?) with a rifle. I lay there for about an hour but we were never mopped up and the exercise, being over, I got back about 4.0 p.m."

He illustrates this letter with 4 sketches, poking fun at himself 1) Side view of a fierce airman looking for enemy 2) Front view of airman from behind bush 3) Front view of airman after first view of enemy from behind long grass 4) Enemy approach. Strategic withdrawal of airman and concludes by writing "Ah me! Ta ta for now – I'll call again."

All I can say is thank goodness German troops never did invade, as I am sure my father would have been mopped up very quickly indeed.

The wireless course now progresses from receivers and transmitters to understanding the Beam Approach.

Moving to Bolton, June 1942

"This is the apparatus in a plane which enables the pilot to fly on a beam and find his way home. It also enables him to land in very foggy weather. There is no secret about it as it was in general use in civilian airlines before the war, so I'll tell you a bit about it. I don't think anyone will court martial me for this little explanation under the Official Secrets Act, do you?"

Having learnt about this, he starts working on special sets for fighter planes, which he describes as a 'knotty problem'. Unfortunately his hopes of being selected as an instructor with progression to the rank of corporal are dashed, because there is only one vacancy and Eric gets it. As usual, it is due to his practical marks not being as good as his theory and although he understands this, he is clearly disappointed.

Eileen spurs him on by suggesting he come for a day to her grandmother's in Liverpool. By now it is August and this visit seems to have done the trick. He writes: "Yesterday seems like a glorious dream – and today I have had to pinch myself to see if I am awake – for my thoughts have been with you all along. It was very thrilling to see you and be with you those five-short but happy hours. I had got so excited about coming that I forgot my gas mask and had to go back for it – then I almost forgot to get a ticket and on arrival at Liverpool I realised I had forgotten to pick up my things and nearly left the train without them. Oh boy, it was exciting and such a burning happiness within me just to be with you again. I am longing for next Saturday. Passes have been extended and I could stay and catch a train about 6.0 am on Monday morning. It would be well worth it, if it does not upset any domestic arrangements."

Moving to Bolton, June 1942

There is quite a lot of German bombing going on over the Lancashire area during this period "German planes zoomed very low over Bolton and flares dropped all around. In the Manchester direction the guns were banging away. Eric and I got up and helped Mrs Mather in street fire-watching, as it was extra lively. I do hope you weren't disturbed, as all the excitement seemed over Liverpool way. I had a cup of tea with Mrs Cunliffe – her husband goes to a warden's post - and she is very scared and can't stand up when there is any noise so I popped in and nattered about Liverpool, trains, church etc and tried to make her laugh – by which time the all clear sounded at 1.20 a.m. There was a mouse in her kitchen – imagine me chasing a mouse behind a sideboard with a poker and an air raid on!"

Somehow David with a poker is a bit more believable than David with a rifle. But he never says whether he actually managed to kill Mighty Mouse.

David always seems to 'enjoy' the war vicariously only from a distance. e.g. he writes at the end of this same letter "This afternoon we were listening to fighter pilots flying over N. Wales - it was very exciting and perfectly clear."

Eileen sounds to have a whole week's holiday at her grandmother's and makes the best of it with a trip to Morecambe and catching up with her sister, Dulcie. Whilst there, a rather eccentric uncle Norman descends upon them and, as she says in a letter home to Mutti Lanc, "honestly we've been laughing ever since; he is more of a scream than ever now he is in the Navy, for instance this morning he came into Dulcie's and my

Moving to Bolton, June 1942

bedroom and kept hitting us and pretending to pull the clothes off. We defended ourselves with pillows and a wire hairbrush, we finally succeeded in forcing him out of the room and barricading the door with an armchair; he then went to torment Mummy, but luckily for her his purpose got deflected on the sight of her corsets lying on the chair, so he put them on over his dressing gown and paraded round the house with them on back to front. He eventually took them off and hung them on the picture rail in the breakfast room."

Slapstick humour of this sort seems to have been a form of release for situations of wartime tension and she goes on to describe how this same uncle got them all doing a Chelsea pensioner bath chair drill because he reckoned they would all be Chelsea pensioners by the time the war finished. She ends her letter cheerily by saying "See if you can get Jerry to wipe out the tax Office in my absence."

The weather is hot and working inside planes even hotter. David records: "We have spent another day in a Hampden – learning how to remove the fruit machine and reinstall it. It does make you hot, bunched into a tiny space and manoeuvring a set in and out. I don't know how the crews ever get out in a hurry, as everywhere seems so confined. All this week we are on 'Aircraft Maintenance' an entirely practical week - we work on actual planes - there are the bodies of Spitfires, Hurricanes, and Wellingtons and the whole day we have been crawling all round them, inside and out, and can find all the wireless equipment by now – besides playing with all the other controls. I spent most of my morning

Moving to Bolton, June 1942

half in and half out of a Spitfire's fuselage, trying to take out and put back a motor generator and in the afternoon was in the pilot's cockpit of a Wellington generally amusing myself."

The accompanying sketches of these say "me getting generator out and getting very hot and red faced due to effort" and "me in Wellington cockpit – supercilious look on face not apparent in sketch."

Towards the end of the course they are moved onto "petrol electric engines – small petrol driven engines driving dynamos – and it is part of our job to understand these things. It has been interesting to learn all about 4 stroke engines, magnets, the carburettor etc. and in fact just what happens in an internal combustion engine. We are also working on a large transmitter which has a 3000 volts supply. Casualties from shock on this thing average one a week in sick quarters, so we have to be careful what we do. Next week we are on American wireless equipment now used in England - revision - then the Board. A fortnight tonight I shall be ringing you up to let you know the result."

His friend, Les, has meanwhile been kicked off the course for not trying hard enough and would be leaving for another drome, so it looked like all change again before too long.

A previous friend from Southend, Les, has been posted abroad and David goes to visit his parents for the weekend in Manchester to catch up on the latest news. "Mr and Mrs Gill are very nice people and I might have been their son the way they looked after me. I learnt lots of news about Les and read a lot of his descriptions.

Moving to Bolton, June 1942

He seems to be having a very nice time out there. They got out there fairly easily but the ship behind theirs in the convoy was torpedoed off Plymouth and they had 5 submarines following them for days. In Durban they had a royal welcome from the people and a wonderful time of sightseeing and entertainment during the 4 days they were there. Grapes are 2½ d per pound!"

Eileen makes the best of the summer with trips with her brother and sister to Cleethorpes and Skegness. It seems as if people were able to enjoy themselves at weekends, despite the wartime conditions. "We got up very early, cut sandwiches etc to last the whole day and then caught the 10 o' clock train. It was a glorious day, so we went straight to the bathing pool; we spent the whole day there, we had bathes and then sunbathed all the time. I plucked up the courage and went down the chute, I quite enjoyed it once I got used to it being so steep. We saw lots of airmen, especially on the boating lake where it was so crowded, on account of only half the lake being used and the whole of the fleet of boats being out. It was fun, one couldn't row more than 4 strokes before colliding and when Norman was rowing, Dulce and I sat one end and weighted it down so much that it stuck on a sandbank and some boys had to tow us off it. It was more like water dodgems."

But the summer is over. The wireless exam took place around 6th September and more moves are now afoot.

8
Moving to SHQ Signals Section RAF Duxford, Nr. Cambridge, Sept 1942

David's first letter from Duxford is extremely positive.

> "Oh boy – I'm bubbling over with delight and satisfaction at what I've seen and heard about this camp up to now – in fact everything has been lovely since leaving home. It is a pre-war camp and is quite luxurious. We live in blocks of flats - well-built places, and the beds are well spread out. Our room is well lighted and we have a table among us. On the same floor are excellent wash places, showers, duck eggs (i.e.toilets) and ample supplies of hot water. After tea, which was bread and butter and fried fish, we all explored the place.

Moving to SHQ Signals Section, RAF Duxford

> At the entrance is a camp P.O. and 2 telephone boxes – I got through to home in 4 mins tonight. Then there is a NAAFI which seems well stocked. Above it there are billiards and table tennis rooms, a reading and writing room and a good library. I noticed classes are held once a week in maths, navigation, French, German and Spanish, so I shall join something there. There is a camp theatre, cinema and dance hall and something on every night – <u>all free.</u> The countryside resembles that round Billingborough - not too flat - and not too near the monotonous marsh and fen land. Saffron Walden is fairly near and is a local beauty spot. Ely and Cambridge are within bounds. I saw Ely cathedral today and it is very beautiful indeed. As far as I can make out, we are attached to SHQ Signals and not to a Squadron. This may mean we are more or less permanent fixtures. I don't mind staying here for a long time. Discipline is negligible – fellows seem to go around dressed as they wish – and wireless mechanics do not parade at all like others do. We just wander to work on our own."

First impressions of the physical place are one thing, but the actual working environment is not so good.

> "Our work is pretty awful – we are all 'cheesed off' because we have done practically nothing, except watch and stand around. We have 3 impossible NCOs – 2 corporals who are very cocky and clever and one Flight Sergeant who is always trying to take the rise out of us – bawls at us, treats us as if we were ignorant and generally makes himself unpleasant. There are sets and jobs which we can tackle with ease, but the moment we touch

Moving to SHQ Signals Section, RAF Duxford

a thing, we are shouted at, told not to play about. Instead we have spent the time carrying things from here to there - do this, do that – get out of the way etc., etc., etc. There is very little for us to do anyway and this endless hanging about knocks all keenness out of you – and the enthusiasm with which I came down seems to be dwindling. The F/S has the annoying habit of laughing, or rather neighing at his own jokes, and the Corporals boast about what they have said and done and bore you stiff. Even if you do something, it is wrong – ah well – having blown off steam, I will pack it up."

Eileen is pondering what she might be doing next. She has signed up for a Church of England confirmation class to start in the autumn and she also wonders about trying to join the WAAFs. David is pleased about the former, but less sure about the latter. He cannot really envisage her fitting in with the WAAF mentality. He explains as follows:

"On Monday night there was an Ensa concert – Noel Coward's 'Private Lives' - a play about the blasé people in the 1922/3 period, all quite humorous, but lots of dirty humour put in unnecessarily. It was quite embarrassing with such a large number of WAAFs there, but I found they did not seem to care – they seem to appreciate it; do you know I find the WAAFs a most peculiar type of woman – very sophisticated and hard in their ways. I just can't picture you among them – your tender ways and feelings just don't fit in and I'm sure you wouldn't feel happy among them."

9
Move to Babraham

What actually happens is that David is quite quickly moved to Babraham which is several miles away from Duxford and is then a lot happier. They are housed in a hut near a Steingot mast and come under the care of a Mrs Mulley at 51 London Road. "One end of the hut is a kitchen and dining room with oil stoves for cooking and an electric pan heater. Through the door you come to the bedroom with 4 beds on each side and a stove in the middle – shelves above the beds and a wireless. We do all our own cooking, except dinner which Mrs Mulley comes in and does with one of us to help. A ration van comes up from Duxford each day and brings our food. There seems plenty to eat and better than Duxford because it is cooked better. I understand we get eggs and milk privately in the village." The routine varies day by day, but for example Thursday involves:

"1) Assist in preparation of breakfast and go on duty at 9.0 a.m. until 5.0p.m. - being relieved for dinner

Move to Babraham

> 2) Have tea and wash up
> 3) Stand by and prepare supper
> 4) Go on duty at 11.0 p.m. until 9.0 a.m. This consists of being on duty, but as the operations room closes down about 11 until about 6.00 a.m. you can sleep on a bed there. There is an electric fire and you can sleep properly in pyjamas. Of course, if there is any flying at night, we have to be up and on watch.
> 5) Friday 9.00 a.m. Come off duty, have breakfast and then free all day except for dinner assistant and room orderly in the morning. This means cleaning up, sweeping and helping Mrs Mulley. Wash up after dinner."

As to the work itself he explains:

> "The receiver station is across a ploughed field about 10 mins walk from here, and it must be weird at night. The sets are in one of those ordinary arch shaped concrete air raid shelters which usually accommodate about 25 people. The sets and main switchboard, electric fire and bed and chair are down there. We are perhaps 6 feet below ground level – get the idea?
>
> All we have to do is watch some receiver sets and listen to conversations between air and ground. Occasionally telephone instructions come through to set up spare receivers to different frequencies. If any receiver conks out, we must get a spare one going <u>immediately</u>, for while a receiver is out of service, planes are out of touch with the ground and can get lost very easily. Then we set to and put the other one right again. Each hour we have to check the tuning needle position, as frequencies drift slightly due to temperature etc.

and you may not be dead on your stations – this is just as bad as breaking down, as if you're off tune, it is very faint! We have a pair of earphones which hear everything said from ground to air and air to ground, and most interesting conversations are heard. If the enemy was around, we should hear the pilot's account of his battle. The rest of the time on duty you read, write etc. I'll tell you more about it all later."

Cambridge is within striking distance of Babraham and it is not long before David decides to cycle over there. "I spent 2 hours in Boots book section and in another bookshop. These shops are crowded with students, some wearing gowns. They all look about my age, are well dressed, and pore over books of philosophy, theology etc. Sh-sh-sh but I must confess I was a wee bit envious and wished I could be at Cambridge with them, learning more and having a good education – always provided the war was over, of course – seeing all these young fellows at college is apt to make me slightly discontented, but I do not dwell on it and just forget it. I should certainly like to send my son (if any) to Cambridge or Oxford. I was in my element in the bookshop and saw all the latest German publications – grammars, readers, colloquial German books etc." As a Grammar school boy David always felt rather in awe of public school types and perhaps these comments are a reflection of the privilege and class difference which he sensed when seeing the university students. Also, of course, at 21 he could feel his youth was passing him by and he did not know how long the war would last or what career prospects he would have post-war. He writes

The billet that Christmas

"I wonder what they <u>will</u> do with us after the war? I don't suppose they will be short of tax inspectors, as they are reserved now anyway. Still, there may be something for us to go at." I think in some ways the RAF was the equivalent of a university because it brought young men with different ideas together and there was a certain camaraderie and shared experience. The billet was the place for debate, discussion and presumably argument, but also the place for relaxation in much the same way as a junior common room might be.

One of his mates in the billet is called Edgar and he produces a very good sketch of what the main room looked like: "it is very typical of an RAF hut (between inspections) and you can see how we arrange our biscuits (i.e. mattresses) and blankets as a chair. You may find also the collar and tie hanging up, respirator and tin hat, odds and ends on shelves and half empty kit bags.

Move to Babraham

Ken is sitting on the bed sewing, our LAC is playing darts and I think it was Mac who was asleep. My bed is the one just behind the dart player."

Cambridge continues to be a draw and sometimes he gets a lift on the back of a motorbike or hitches. He is impressed by the Evensong of Kings College chapel. "Nothing can change what time has moulded in such a place. That is the wonderful feeling you get during a service there. It does restore one's mental balance of everything." Other times he is more down to earth and goes to do shopping for the lads – tobacco, batteries etc. "and then I had a haircut, a bath in the public baths, had dinner, bought some pears, went to the flicks and fed my face with the aforementioned pears." Another time in the early Autumn he takes a canoe out on the backs and sends a long descriptive letter all about what he can see from this angle.

> "There are some lovely weeping willows on each side of the river, casting cool shadows into the water – parklands, shady paths, wooded copses and the stately college buildings. Straight ahead is St Johns – a wonderful building, covered with red and green ivy – its cloisters, towers and spires show up among the trees and fields surrounding it. From St Johns is the old Bridge of Sighs, connecting two halves of the college on either side of the river and as you row under the bridge, college walls tower over you on both sides and you feel as if you're in a castle moat. On my right is Kings College and its beautiful chapel with lovely sculptured towers on each corner, like minarets. It is just as beautiful inside, with fan laced roof, stately pillars

Move to Babraham

> and old oak choir stalls. I <u>do</u> wish you were here and could see this with me. I am sure together, here we should find perfect peace."

On that same occasion he ends up having tea with the Kings college chaplain whom he meets quite by chance when looking round a different church. "Halfway through the tea a WAAF turned up from a neighbouring drome. She apparently was in the chaplain's old parish once upon a time, and had come to see him, so she had tea. She was a very attractive blonde with lipstick and goo-goo eyes. OOO er!!! Then the chaplain put on his gown and mortar board and we all proceeded to evensong. Unfortunately he had got the wrong day – Sat evensong starts next week – he was very sorry, but I have his card and can go and see him anytime. Then I went to the YM for some more tea – you know what these afternoon teas with clergymen are, and set off back to Babraham."

For a Yorkshire boy who had grown up in a mining town, one can detect that he is quite overawed by Cambridge and found it a wonderful place to visit on his days off.

David's letters seem to oscillate between the sublime and the ridiculous. In the very same letter as he has waxed lyrical about Cambridge, he descends to the lavatorial. Apparently there was no mains toilet in the hut, only an Elsan "re: duck eggs – there ain't one out here on the station and it's back to Nature once again. Keep it dark, but I've already nettled myself in an awkward spot!!" They snaffle 4 new toilet rolls from Duxford when they collect their week's laundry and hide them amongst

Move to Babraham

the washing. It seems as if up to that point they had to "stoop as low as the Daily Mirror and the Radio Times."

The men seem to have got Elsan on the brain because they set up an 'Elsan fund'. He explains that each person pays 2/6d per week.

> "This supplies 1 pint of milk, sometimes 2 pints per day above the RAF ration which comes in tins. It also supplies 3 newspapers Daily Telegraph, Mail and Mirror and pays Mrs Mulley to come in and cook dinner each day. It is a private arrangement with her and is not an official RAF idea. The surplus cash buys fruit and eggs in the village and cakes from the YMCA van which comes round twice a week. One may also borrow from the fund when an expensive train journey is necessary, if one wishes. What do you think of all this?"

It seems that David is:

> "promoted to treasurer of the Elsan fund, owing to the posting of one of the fellows back to Duxford. Apart from keeping accounts, the spending of the money rests with me and I have more or less a free hand. People come along with ideas of things we need – pan-scraper-outer dishcloth affair on a stick etc. I snoop around buying tomatoes, fish pastes, eggs (sometimes) and when the YMCA van comes, I buy cakes, jam rolls, biscuits and also quantities of cigs and choc, chewing gum and matches for sale to the fellows. They come to me for small loans, stamps etc. You can see I'm very busy with it."

The obsessional detailed account keeping was right

Move to Babraham

up David's street and shows how really he would have been better employed on an admin/clerical job in the RAF.

Eileen back in Louth has had some developments. She receives a first-class typing award in her exam which she is very pleased about, but as regards being called up into the WAAFs she writes: "We have had some more instructions about the Call Up and Miss Parkinson as Grade 3 Temp will be released; Clerical assistants will also, but those who are Allowance Holders will not; therefore I 'stay put' at present." She rather dismisses David's objections to her entering the WAAFs because she feels that there is bound to be a cross-section of people there and she would be able to find some like-minded friends amongst them. But for the time being it is not likely to be an option anyway. She has needlessly put herself through the inoculation process, cycled 5 miles to the doctor's twice and given herself a cold into the bargain, all for nothing!

Her confirmation classes seem to be providing her with much food for thought and she describes the subjects at length to David in a letter dated 20.10.42. She looks forward to a time when they will both be able to go up to the communion rail together and she hopes David will be able to attend her confirmation service on 26th November to be performed by the Bishop of Lincoln in St. James' church, Louth. The Rev. Everard Evans is the minister who takes the classes and she seems to have a lot of respect for him, although she is quite willing to challenge his views on Wesley: "Being brought up a Wesleyan you can understand that I had

Move to Babraham

some criticism of some of the ideas the Vicar put forth; he for instance, was inclined to condemn Wesley without acknowledging that his mission was only brought about by the decaying state of the Church of England at that time, and the need of the big industrial masses for a spiritual leader to help them in their hard daily lives and to improve their appalling working conditions."

For me it is interesting to read about Rev Everard Evans because much later on (1951) when David and Eileen wanted me to be christened and they were living in Kent, he was the vicar of Bexley and so they linked up with him again.

Life at Babraham was good on the whole, but it had its frustrations. For example one Sunday turned out to be a complete fiasco:

> "When I arrived on duty, I found two fellows doing some intercomm wiring job so we can have an intercomm system with the girls in the 'cabins' in the operations room. You see, each receiver is on a particular channel and goes to a particular cabin. The controller instructs the girls what to reply to planes and they also log everything they hear and reply. Well, these two fellows nattered and swore all the day, upset the peace of the place, and continually kept knocking plugs out at the back of the sets. Of course the first I knew of it was a snorting bloke from operations, wanting to know why a set was 'off the air'? I had to report why, got a chewing up, and in turn had to chew them up mildly and thus created a bad atmosphere. The same happened again and in the end I had to sit with the earphones continually on, which is very trying, in order to detect as soon as a plug came

out. They also messed up the phone and I was unable to contact the outside world for 2 hours. Today poor old Mac is on watch with them and there has been in RAF language 'bags of panic'. Sets off the air, due to their wiring and soldering their wires near the receiver lines, planes up and a couple of channels out of order, and in addition some Jerries in the area and not a spare channel to work fighters on. The two workable channels were leaking into one another, so that what was said on each channel was coming through on both and girls were logging two channels, not knowing which was which! The controller has been tearing his hair this morning and there will be a bust up shortly! It is the wiring party to blame and not us at all. To crown all yesterday, when I was getting crosser and crosser with everything, I went off watch at 11.0 p.m. and was just in bed, when there was some night flying – I had to return and was at it until 1.15 a.m. - then up at 5.0 am again this morning – I bust my wrist watch too - and then on orderly this morning I had to mend the vacuum cleaner which stopped the job and the electric fire yesterday. I had to mend 3 times or starve in the cold. What a chapter of accidents!"

The correspondence between David and Eileen is increasingly a sounding board for ideas, a place to blow off steam or a means of confiding more intimate feelings, allowing for greater vulnerability as confidences are revealed. Each of them is able to reflect their hopes and fears in letter writing and there is a simple honesty about the way they correspond. David thinks back to the time when he went to be prepared for confirmation with his priest Rev. Pawson. He would have only been

Move to Babraham

aged about 12, it seems, and must have been very naive in his approach to life. He recalls:

> "We had such grand talks and he used to help me a lot. He helped me to understand how I was born and began the story and led up to being christened. I must have been a strange child – I know I was very credulous and believed in Father Xmas until I was 11, and had to be told so that I shouldn't be laughed at. I believed babies were put together by doctors and even when I was 12 and went to see an aunt at the nursing home, I had great hopes in seeing arms and legs on a tray ready to be made"

It seems unbelievable to us nowadays that a child could be kept in the dark for so long as regards the facts of life, but even Eileen, growing up on a dairy farm as she did, was never allowed to witness a cow giving birth to a calf. The pre-war years were obviously very different from the post war years in terms of people's openness on all manner of topics. Children who grew up during the war presumably could no longer be shielded from life's harsher realities and so the war marked a turning point in how people were forced to communicate. David and Eileen's correspondence, although increasingly open and frank, does have a certain quaintness about it which shows them up more as pre-war children with a less sophisticated view of life.

Some social niceties and corners are being knocked off as they experience more of the 'big wide world', but on the whole these two 21yr olds seem quite young for their age, still able to get pleasure from simple things

Move to Babraham

and easily overawed by new experiences. In that sense their letters are innocent and endearing. The office rules of social behaviour are also relaxing as a result of war. Eileen writes: "About nine o' clock tonight I heard strains of 'Good King Wenceslas' outside the office door and went down to find Brailsford and Betha there, they had come to play table tennis; we had some good games; really you wouldn't recognise your dignified, prim and proper office, now that it is overrun with girls laughing and dashing about. We got teased in the tea room the other day because Parky happened to mention that we wear curlers when we are firewatching. They asked us what we should do if we wanted our tin hats on; women at war!"

David agrees that the formality of the pre-war office must have changed considerably since he left it: "maybe I wouldn't recognise the office which was so prim and proper – but that's a good thing. I think fire watching has improved the relationships between office staff – they all get to know one another better. Maybe you wouldn't recognise your prim and proper Tax Officer who used to say Good Morning so sweetly to all the taxpayers and rush about for confounded taxpayers' files." So he is conscious that the RAF has changed him too and that the old civilities are dying as the war progresses.

The war seems to be turning a little more in favour of the Allies at this point and there is intensive training of pilots. David recognises a Flight Sergeant Squires from Leicester when he is in Cambridge and this man informs him that there is a pilot's course at St Johns university with thousands being trained. Back at the billet there is

Move to Babraham

avid following of the news bulletins. David writes:

> "The news is wonderful and ever so cheering. Last night's news affected everyone here so much that we couldn't go to sleep for a long time. At last we are winning and can see the end in the distance. The immediate psychological effect on myself of all this wonderful news is that I forget such trivialities as leave, time off, and feel I can go on working and working. I feel I wouldn't mind if I were sent to Algeria tomorrow to be part of all these great events. Our turn may come when we invade across the Channel. What do you all think of the news? Time seems endless between news bulletins."

There is another practical exam plus an oral to be overcome back at Duxford. Three of them set off early one morning but they only have 2 bikes, so attempt to carry one man on the cross bar instead. David is not in very good form, having blister burns on his fingers, a painful abscess on his gum (which has been festering for a while) and a 10 day old ear infection. There were no antibiotics and so he just treated the ears with olive oil, peroxide and deep breathing. He is down to have an X ray of the gum at Cambridge Hospital and sounds generally out of sorts. He needs to pass each section of the exam with over 60% in order to become an A/C1.

Doing night watches seems to be taking up the majority of his time: "At night we have the machine gun at the side, loaded, with 2 spare magazines of rounds each, lying within easy reach. Very often I have the drill on my own – by imagining noise, dashing up with the gun, and shooting the enemy. Sometimes I include loading as part of the drill! I believe in theory I have to ring up the Signals Officer for permission to fire – so you would have to wait a few minutes before being shot!"

On a lighter note he talks about how 3 of the men decided to:

> "clean out the pantry and got a system going. Things were in different tins, some were old and unrecognisable, so we conveniently lost them. Sam put a tin of old curry in the pig bin and then worried all night lest 'Old Mulley's pigs' caught pneumonia by eating curry. Everything now organised, labels on each tin, all empty ones stuck away, shelves cleaned and labels on the front of the shelf, wherever milk and butter and so on have to be put. I scrubbed the floor – it is rough concrete and in one corner where the veg and water pails stand, it was filthy. There was a thickness of earth mould, decayed brussels sprouts and splashed water – all combined to create a drain smell. It was this smell which started us on the job. Then going round with the vac, Sam got a brussels sprout up the tube - it zoomed up into the bag, making a most peculiar noise. Our vac is a sucker and a blower – I got the blower end on accidentally and blew a shower of custard powder everywhere. To finish up, here is a sketch of self, challenging enemy at the door of my shelter."

If this was the best he could do with a hoover, I hate to think what would have happened if he had used the machine gun against the enemy.

One night he was more realistically put to the test:

Move to Babraham

"Last night I went on duty and had got over to receivers when John and I, who was relieving him, saw a light down the field path. It was eerie, and we were somewhat perturbed. John cycled back and I loaded the Tommy gun, drew back the bolt, and it was all ready for firing. Then I stood in the doorway and watched for about 10 mins and saw the light again. I locked myself in the place and rang up to see whether John had arrived - he had and said he had heard scuffling in the hedge near the path as he rode past. He and Cliff had decided to investigate, by walking up to the receivers on the other side of the hedge. I went out again with my gun, but saw nothing, and they arrived and said they had seen nothing either. Back they went and I got ready for bed and rang Edgar on transmitters for a chat. While I was talking to him, I thought I heard the door knob being turned and strained hard to listen and seemed to hear all sorts of noises. It is an awful sensation - I could feel my heart bumping away inside me, and felt very uncomfortable – I heard nothing eventually

Move to Babraham

> and after a consoling natter to Edgar, I shut out all noises and went to sleep. I laugh about it now when I think of it, but must say I was very keyed up. Thus ends my ghost story!"

He is altogether happier doing domestic duties in the billet. "I was on dinner today and made cottage pie and peas and as a sweet I cored some apples, but not right through – put a spoon of treacle in, stuffed them with raisins and covered the top of the hole with margarine. They turned out very nice and were well enjoyed." David knows he is well off at Babraham, especially compared with his friend Alwyn, who has been posted to Surrey "where he is living a hard, active service life living in a tent with 4 blankets, the NAAFI cafes etc. out of bounds, mail about once a fortnight - works 2 days and does fatigues the 3rd day, lives on dog biscuits, canned bacon, corned beef and soup."

Eileen too has her share of night time noises to report to match David's account:

> "We got on all right fire watching on Tuesday night, we worked till ten o' clock and then had supper and packed off to sleep; it's funny there are most weird noises in the office at night all the radiators and pipes contract and clank at intervals. Parky gets quite worried and says 'Oh, what's that, should we lock the door?' I take my breakfast and have it at the office to save time in the morning. I can then start at 8 a.m. instead of nine. Parky teases me when I'm making the porridge by calling me 'mother'. I do have to look after her, though, tuck her in bed at night and put chairs alongside to keep her from falling out. I shall be

quite sorry when she joins up because we get on well together."

The weekend of the confirmation arrives and David is able to get leave for what Eileen calls 'three days of heaven', which incorporates not only the service, but also a dance. He has had the offending tooth removed and the abscess has cleared up, so he is in good form. It is a long time since they have seen one another and everything comes up to expectation. However, when he gets back to camp, he finds that 3 of his mates Mac, Dan and Sam have gone, without warning.

They have been posted to Driffield on a squadron and "may be overseas in no time." Apparently, David would also have had to go if he had not been on leave and Sam has gone in his place. It is quite a "shock to find them gone and you have never even said goodbye." Cliff and Edgar are still in the same billet and Edgar has wangled it that while he is on transmitters, David is on receivers, so this seems to work well.

The night duty in the hut affords plenty of time for reading and writing and it is interesting to see what kind of subjects occupy David at this point of late 1942. He writes: "I have spent a quiet day on watch writing a long letter home and divided the rest of my time digesting the Beveridge plan, about which I am not much wiser, although it is a grand scheme. The rest of the time I have wrestled with an algebra problem and got into a terrible mess." Unfortunately he has not passed his wireless exam high enough to be an AC/1 and so is a bit unsure of what to do next. Eileen, for her part, is exploring all the possible duties which are available in

Move to Babraham

the WAAFs. She is quite interested in the 'plotters' which comes under 'Clerks Special Duties'. Alternatively there are meteorologist jobs and she asks David to research what these duties entail. She sends him an introductory pamphlet and he replies:

> "I would suggest you put Clerk Special Duties first yourself as preference. You will then get into operations in both Bomber command or Fighter Command.
>
> The different jobs in operations, such as plotters, etc. are all clerk SD and I think you would like this best. As regards meteorologist, it depends where you are put - if you are on a met station, you may be out in the wilds and of course have to carry out weather tests, send up balloons etc. in most shocking weather. Or you may be put in met office attached to operations. Here you get weather reports coming through the teleprinter machines in code from different met stations and have to file them and each hour make your observations of the local weather. I am told it is rather boring and monotonous. As for clerk/general duties, this is nothing more than a form-filler-upper, typing etc. and I should avoid it if you can. You come into contact with the common airman more in this job and any tin pot office girl can manage this job. It is not good enough for you and you will like operations much better. The RTOs are the cabin girls as you suggest – don't go for this at all!
>
> Of course I must warn you that whatever job you get, it is bound to be boring occasionally, although in print it's attractive. Jobs have been divided and cut down to one single thing so much

that it is bound to be cheesing at times. Even ours is sometimes! If you get into operations or met you will get all hours of duty which the clerks GD don't get – but you will like it best and find a nicer kind of girl there. I hope I don't seem to be preaching at you dear, but I want you to get where you would be happiest and with the better class girl."

Looking at this letter now, it comes across as quite class conscious and condescending in its tone. One wonders too, whether he is afraid of her meeting a 'common airman' who might pose some competition to him.

It may all be academic because, as Eileen points out in her next letter, although the Civil Service "might allow people to volunteer to be released for the services, the snag is that we shall not be able to volunteer in the Ministry of Labour sense because we have already registered; we consequently would merely be conscripted and have no choice." Nonetheless, she starts working independently on reading up about meteorology because "the information might be valuable if I was given a test before being put on the course. I don't think there is anything I could study in connection with the plotters work, is there? "

Christmas is fast approaching and she is more concerned with presents and parties. Unable to find any book tokens in town, she ends up sending a postal order so that David will be able to buy something in Cambridge. She herself wants a reference book on British statesmen, but suggests it should be a Xmas-cum-birthday present, as books are so hard to come by.

Move to Babraham

The girls' office party:

> "was lovely. We had a gramophone which enabled us to waltz round Bowder's cupboard, down to the open space near the filing room door and finally, through good manipulating, to end up with a good spin near Mr Taylor's desk. We also had an American table tennis tournament, it was good fun; and we mustn't forget the eats, we each brought something and it was amazing the spread we got, we set it all out along Bowder's and Crawley's desks and it stretched the whole length, there were 46 small cakes and pastries, sandwiches, and tomatoes, chocolate roll, apple pie and tea to drink; we said Bowder would be finding crumbs in the nicks and crannies of his desk and dusting for all he was worth the next day. All the girls thoroughly enjoyed themselves, we packed up at 10.30. Then Parky and I cleared up and Parky found she had put the hot teapot down on Uncle Bowder's desk and made a big ring on the green leather part, we tried to cover it with green ink as it had taken the colour out, but after getting the stuff all over our hands, we decided it was no improvement, so just had to leave it exposed to Uncle Herbert's critical gaze. However, we put his post over it in the morning and he didn't notice it."

The formality of the pre-war office certainly had changed and it was largely due to the influx of female staff, who were beginning to assert themselves and enjoy themselves.

David knows he will be staying in camp for Christmas and not going home to Barnsley until 8th

Move to Babraham

January. He resolves meanwhile to find out more detail about jobs in the WAAFs and has a private conversation with a corporal to get inside information. He cautions Eileen to keep it under her hat as it should really be kept confidential within the Forces:

> "the meteorological girls are apparently a section on their own, whereas clerk S.D. come under operations and is not such a small independent unit. Your different jobs are as follows:-
>
> 1) To go out every hour and make a general report on the weather – wind speeds, cloud heights, type of cloud etc.
>
> 2) To compare local weather with a neighbouring station's met girl
>
> 3) To send off in code, by teleprinter, a weather report to Met HQ Fighter Commander
>
> 4) The whole time, a teleprinter is sending out sheets and sheets of weather reports of the whole country, from some central place. An automatic teleprinter at this place types out the weather and as it is being typed there, it appears on the teleprinter machines in every met office. It is all in code of course. Every so often you tear off a few feet of weather reports and pin them up on the wall, so that if at any time ops want to know the weather round Newcastle or Plymouth, you refer to your sheet, translate the code and proudly say 'Oh, it's drizzling slightly and there is cloud at 3000ft - very little wind.
>
> I believe I was wrong when I said you were on outstations – you are nearly always on a drome."

Move to Babraham

He goes on to describe the work of the Plotters.

> "Standing round the main table, on which is a huge map of the area, there may be about a dozen of you, each with a small area. Every <u>plane</u> – your own station's, every bomber passing over and every enemy plane is put on the map, and you push them around - together with details regarding their type, height, speed etc. - all this gen comes from the Observer Corps. Hence the Controller can see at a glance just what he wants to know about every plane.
>
> There are the 'Tellers' who pass on gen from Observer Corps to the girls on the table and report the precise position of our own planes. The tellers get their information of our own fighters' positions from the girls in the triangulator room – here 3 girls sit round a circular table on which is a map of the area all marked off in degrees of latitude and longitude. Each has a string, one end of which is fastened to a place on the board where a wireless direction-finding station is situated. When a plane transmits, to find its position, 3 DF stations locate it along a certain bearing – each station reports that bearing and you lay your string along the bearing that your DF station has given. Where the 3 strings intersect is the position of the plane – which is given to the tellers."

The corporal has also commented that "the better type of girl, mostly school cert, hold the met and ops room jobs and they are usually a good crowd."

He certainly leaves Eileen with plenty to think about over Christmas and she in turn discusses with her parents the idea of joining up, in case the office is willing to release her in future.

Move to Babraham

As the holiday season approaches:

> "The greatest excitement at Babraham is a group of Italian prisoners working in the fields next to our hut. They exhibit great interest in our aerials and seem quite friendly. One of them, sitting on the roadside called out to me 'Pleece times pleece' so I told him and he understood. They wander around as they wish and their one soldier guard ignores them most of the time. You often pass one or two hunting for rabbits. Bill and Ken were walking back today from receivers, carrying a set which had broken down, when they passed four Italians, each with a curved shaped knife (used for cutting swedes in the field) and a dirty look on their faces. They properly had the wind up, as if 4 of them were suddenly to go patriotic, they might do anything! Most of them give us a grin or thumbs up sign which we return. They are always singing in the field"

Although he makes light of this incident, it seems to have played on his mind a bit because he writes in his next letter "I have been having tommy gun practice with myself this morning, and if I were to hear a sound now, I could put down this letter and be firing at the rate of 700 rounds a minute within a couple of seconds, so why should I worry?"

The huts at Babraham were isolated and miles from the main camp at Duxford, so perhaps the men felt more vulnerable. Christmas too was a rather dismal affair because David was on duty in the 'crypt' from 5-11 Xmas eve, 9-5 Xmas Day and again at 11 p.m. on Xmas night. This meant long hours alone. He cheered himself up by bringing over an old battery wireless so he could

Move to Babraham

listen to some programmes and "had a party with a piece of cake, some licquorice allsorts and an apple."

The other chaps were able to celebrate having a dinner of turkey and pork in the billet plus Xmas pud made by Mrs Mulley and although eventually David got back for the same food in the afternoon, he had to eat it on his own. Boxing Day made up for it all, however. "I had a really grand time and thoroughly let myself go" he explains. He and Edgar go over to a family at Sawston, whom they have got to know.

> "When we arrived, we sang a carol at the front door and then dashed round to the French windows and held out our caps, for those in the room to fork out! We had a merry party - Mr and Mrs Allen and their 2 nieces Elsa and Hilda (aged

The billet at Babraham with David at the front

approx 30-33) who work in London. Edgar had thought out a list of games and we split into pairs, each played a different game and then passed it on. We had to pick up dried peas with knitting needles, matches with a pin, work out some jumbled names - each game lasted 3 mins. We played beetles and 'passing the bottle' where each places the match on the bottle neck and passes it on. You get a very precarious pile of matches and if you knock any off, you add them to your stock."

The food seems to have been plentiful "We had a lovely supper – pork pie and tangerine trifle and Xmas cake and a real egg made sponge cake. After supper we played bagatelle and finally returned about midnight."

And so another whole year has passed and they both wonder what 1943 will bring. David regards Babraham as the best of his RAF life to date, he is glad not to have been posted abroad like some of his friends and he recalls with thankfulness all the good highlights of 1942 when he sends his New Year's Eve letter to Eileen, finishing up by saying "God bless you always and keep you safe."

10
Babraham continued, 1943

David is coming to the realisation that Eileen may well be in the Forces herself before too long. He can appreciate how coming up against a variety of people has broadened his outlook on life and he now is more willing to let Eileen do the same, whereas before he was rather protective. He recommends a particular book to her which is about slum life "You might be shocked if you read it, although I always like to feel you are so broad-minded, you are never shocked. That's the spirit in which to join the WAAFs, and if I had been a bit older and more broadened in outlook, I should never have had my shaking when I joined the RAF." The last two years have in many ways been an eye-opener to him. He seems more sure of his relationship too and although not formally engaged, he makes reference in

Babraham continued, 1943

January 43 to a time 'when we are married'. They have a short holiday break with his parents in Barnsley and this seems to cement things further. "We had such a grand time didn't we? After you went away, you still seemed to be here - sitting at the table or playing the piano. And all the streets echoed your presence – as I deliberately retraced my steps over the paths we took – I could see your happy face as you were on the sledge."

Yet each realises they could end up further away from one another geographically, especially if Eileen does become a meteorologist in the WAAFs. Letters continue to be the mainstay, as Eileen's says "I love writing you letters, it gives me a nice feeling of 'All's right with the world'."

But the war goes on and unexpected things can happen. David is quietly writing a letter one day, when he suddenly breaks into his train of thought: "Great excitement! Just five minutes ago I stopped writing this to watch a barrage balloon which had broken loose and was sailing over towards us about 60 feet up. The next thing was all the lights failed and all our sets went off – the railing wires have cut the mains supply which comes on telegraph posts over the field. All hands to the pump and within 2 minutes we had our emergency petrol engine running and are on emergency mains now - the aircraft up above must have had an unhappy 2 mins without contact with the ground. This is the most interesting thing that has happened for a while. Meanwhile, the old balloon is sailing away and must be heading toward Newmarket."

Eileen can also at times get caught up in war excitement

Babraham continued, 1943

"We had a great thrill yesterday at lunch time when we heard a terrific roar in the air, rushed out to see fourteen flying fortresses in formation heading SW. We heard on the news, of course, that they had made a daylight raid on Wilhelmshaven; that would be the first and not the last American raid on Germany; we really seem to have got Jerry shaking in his shoes."

The tide of the war seems to be turning now and a lot of it was due to the fact that the Americans had been fully drawn in. David writes in January 1943 "What do you think of all the good news? How short a time it seems since at el Alamein we were wishfully thinking of the day we should get Tripoli. As for Russia, no praise is too great for her – and she is a country we must cooperate with much more fully after the war. A mild form of Communism wouldn't do this country any harm – and all these vested interests etc etc want washing out. But how I wonder, also, can British workers have all this admiration for Russian workers and persist in their strikes? I find most Servicemen very bitter about this."

By February Eileen seems clearer about being released from the Civil Service to join up. "It is subject to 3 conditions; one that the Labour Exchange can supply a substitute, two that I pass the medical and three that I am allowed to enter the Service I want to join. So I do, by volunteering, get my choice, which is a great consideration." - David now urges her on "The main thing is for things to move quickly so that vacancies in the trade do not fill up." She is offered a medical at Grimsby for 8th March followed by an interview with the Recruiment Officer. What follows is one of the most

Babraham continued, 1943

indignant letters Eileen has yet been known to write:

> "Well, Laddie, I'm afraid I had a rotten time on Monday; I passed the medical A1, but the interview I had with the WAAF officer afterwards was hopeless, she was a dreadful person with no tact at all, she merely wanted to assert her authority and be domineering the whole time. For instance, she started by asking what qualifications I had, of course I said 'A secondary education and Matric' 'Oh no I don't mean that' so I thought she must want to know what kind of work I did, so I told her I was in the Inspector of Taxes office - 'No, no I don't mean that'. 'Please tell me exactly what you do mean'. I told her I wanted to go in for meteorolgy to which she said irritably 'Oh impossible, you need to have had previous training for that.' I said that I understood there was a course for it – she got very annoyed and said 'There are no vacancies in Met anyway. There are only 2 trades open - Flight mechanics and Wireless Ops'. I told her that I didn't think I was fitted for a Mechanic – she said 'I'm here to tell you what you are suited for, I think you are altogether too bombastic'! I told her I was volunteering and wanted some choice 'You are not volunteering, you are a conscript and have come here under the Nat. Reg. Act.' I replied that I may have come under that act, but the fact remained that I was volunteering. 'I don't like your attitude' she proclaimed, 'we will consider this interview at a close.' I said 'I regard it as far from concluded, we haven't decided anything yet.' I went on to ask her whether there would be any vacancies later on for Met. Girls – she hastily replied 'I've already told you 3 times and I should have thought for

Babraham continued, 1943

an intelligent girl you would have taken it in by now. There will <u>never</u> be any more jobs open for Met. Girls'. Isn't it all absolutely absurd, she had no idea how to interview, it seems terrible that the decision rests with such a 'fool', you can call her nothing else; she could never of heard of such a thing as 'helpful advice', psychology or anything else. There were no office jobs from which I could have re-mustered even. The Flight Mechanic's work must be very interesting, but I don't like the idea of wearing overalls and crawling under planes amidst oil and grease all day, would you? And Wireless Ops is a very monstrous job tapping out Morse. I told Mr Riordan all about the interview, he was very amazed, and now Mr Harrison has received the papers from Grimsby and the old girl has reported 'Refused admission to the WAAF', so Mr Riordan says I will have to choose between joining the ATS or staying at the office. If I join the ATS I shall only do office work, so I think I shall be much more use staying here where I am trained for the work. I've just been unlucky because the WAAF is practically closed."

She is very shocked at the way she has been treated and David tries to suggest various avenues she could go down for advice, including the MP for Louth or writing to the Air Ministry! But in the end he agrees "I should stay put, rather than do a less valuable job in the ATS than you are doing now." She later reports "Mr Riordan and the Inspector were very pleased that I had decided to stay because they are so short of trained staff, so I was quite satisfied to stay where I was useful and where I was wanted. Mr Riordan thinks I am much more use to the War Effort at the office. So I have now mastered that

Babraham continued, 1943

thwarted feeling and have reconciled myself to working out tax liabilities instead of examining the clouds!"

Still, Spring is on its way. David is due to visit her in early April and she looks forward to cycle rides in the country "it helps a lot sometimes to forget this dreadful war and visualise a world at peace and think of all the lovely places you want to go to."

David has meanwhile had a lucky encounter which makes him feel the world is not such a bad place after all. He and a mate called Johnny had one day been going to get the bus to Cambridge, but missed it by 100 yds:

> "we stood there, cursing our luck, until a car, with label DOCTOR on the windscreen, pulled up. I stared hard at the driver as he started up and said 'You're Dr Williamson aren't you'. He looked very amazed, stared at me and said 'Good Lord. Young Laws!' He must have a wonderful memory, considering all the faces he sees. He used to live at the bottom of Kensington Road, Barnsley on our side and was our family doctor from 1926–36. Apart from being a GP, he was ear, nose and throat specialist, took out my tonsils, knew all about my ears etc. In 1936 he went to S.Africa and is now back as Medical Officer of Health for Cambridge and Newmarket. He lives out in the country about 10 miles from here. He seemed delighted to see me, asked about my ears and my RAF medicals and wanted to know all about the family. He gave me his address and telephone number and told me to go and see him for sure. Wasn't this an adventure?"

On the strength of this, David later visits Dr

Babraham continued, 1943

Williamson in his 450 yr old house at Withersfield and has a marvellous time "It is just like a home in *Ideal Homes* magazine, he showed us around his lovely big garden and also showed us his 'gadgets' which he says 'tickle him to death'. He has a little oil vapourising engine in a shed, which provides electricity to some huge accumulators which in turn supply the lighting to the house. It can be switched over to work a pump and if he runs it for 10 mins, it pumps up a day's supply of water. He also has a boiler which supplies central heating to the house. Then we had a nice tea, where a discussion on the tortured peoples of Europe, and the Beveridge report developed. After tea, we sat round the fire and Dr W said 'Let's work up Kensington Rd on your side and down the other and see how many people I can remember. It was great fun to see his face light up when he remembered someone. Oh boy, oh boy! I feel so thrilled about it all." It seems that faith in humanity is restored by this chance encounter and the opportunity to reminisce is very much valued by both parties.

Trips by bike into the surrounding countryside are quite frequent at this time. He thoroughly enjoys an outing to Saffron Walden in mid-March and passes near Debden aerodrome "which figured in the battle of Britain." Eileen thinks nothing of cycling back from Elkington at 11.0 p.m. because "everywhere was simply bathed in moonlight, the 'hollow' looked ever so pretty with the long shadows which the trees cast across the road, there was mist rising from the valley further on and St Mary's lane looked so peaceful with its tall still trees and the spire in the background." The trouble is that she

Babraham continued, 1943

has heard that David might be posted overseas and so

> "All these scenes conjured up many memories, David, of the grand times we had together and I'm afraid I felt very sad when I first thought about them all, and wished you were here desperately, and almost prayed you wouldn't be sent away just yet, as you said you might be last night. Then I remembered Churchill's speech which I had listened to about an hour ago, how he urged us all on to the great tasks which lie ahead before we can have visions of peaceful days again and I realised how brave you were in seeing your duty so clearly and I was then resolved to try with all my might to accept whatever comes as cheerfully as you do and we will both pray and have faith in God's protection, won't we dearest?"

As it happened, all the rumours of overseas postings came to nothing and they were able to meet up as planned, in April before he also had a week's leave in Barnsley.

By this time the Americans were beginning to dominate the camp at Duxford "The Yanks are taking over everything but Signals and Ops - I have been to camp this morning and there are Yank dentists, medical staff etc. and only about 200 RAF there altogether. As from Sat we are going to have American rations (bags of hamburgers) our NAAFI has closed and we come under the American Red Cross for that – we are putting in for a radiogram, a refrigerator and an electric cooking ring. If we stay any length of time, life here should be OK under these new conditions." A few weeks later one of the Signals Sergeants brings up the American Signals

Babraham continued, 1943

Officer from Duxford to Babraham and:

> "explained to him in as complicated a way as possible what our stuff did etc. and told him the chaps up here had all been here quite a time and were very efficient and experienced in the job etc, etc. The American S/O said they had none of this equipment in America and it was new to him and he seemed very impressed by it all and said 'I don't want my chaps to take this over' - he thought it better we should stay and I hope he has mentioned it to the right authorities. Our Sgt thinks we shall be here till July, at least."

The leave in Barnsley provides some light relief and David seems to have used it to let off steam or nervous energy. He recounts

> "I have done the craziest things since I came here and must be the despair of the family. I have been 'playing gorillas' in preparation for guerilla warfare and have terrified Helena and Mary. I hoisted mother to the rack last night and threatened my father with the same and after much struggling, had him up there as well – you should hear the yell mother gives when you let her down over your head! Then I did some gardening – I watered the evergreens in the front garden, wearing my father's bowler hat - the ambulance is coming up for me any day now."

Easter is by now approaching and Eileen has her sister Dulcie to stay for a week in Louth. Her letter of 12th April intermingles the everyday with war events:

Babraham continued, 1943

> "on Saturday afternoon we went to Grimsby and scouted round the wool shops and finally tracked to earth some AB wool, we were lucky to get it, as it's pure wool and very scarce. We went to Cleethorpes 'To see the sea and what did we see?' Well, we saw a terrific explosion on the sands first of all, it turned out to be a mine which was being exploded. At first we thought it was a bomb. That bit of excitement over, we went to the Old Barn Cafe for tea, it was very nice there, especially the beans on toast and cakes."

As for many Britons, a cup of tea seems to be a calming factor and certainly this proved to be the case for the rest of Eileen's life!

She and her sister continue to enjoy things whenever they can and spend the rest of the time there "fitting long dance dresses on and choosing which they are going to wear for the big dance on Wed." They also go to an opera 'Tom Jones' put on by the Grimsby Choral Society with 80 performers in total.

Yet ordinary items seem to be in short supply. For example notepaper and especially envelopes. David says he is "going to start a great envelope salvage campaign" which will involve gumming over the previous address and reusing the envelope several times. Suddenly he sends her a letter, with a new address on it. He thought he was staying put at Babraham until July, but finds out they are moving to Gransden RAF station near Sandy, Bedfordshire.

11
Move to Gransden, Bedfordshire, April 1943

"I arrived at the <u>nearest</u> station – Gamlingay - which is 4 miles from here and was lucky enough to get a lift immediately on an otherwise deserted, winding road which brought me to camp about 10.30 am. It is very isolated from railway stations and main roads. The nearest main lines are at Sandy and St. Neots, two places on the Peterborough line. This camp is spread over miles of fields from the guard room and other usual camp institutions. Our living site is some 15 mins walk across a couple of fields. Fortunately this site is in the cookhouse direction and it is 6 mins walk to there. In two days I have almost walked my legs off. Up to now there is only a handful of people here and there is very little organisation yet. I found my hut – built for about 30 and there are only 9 or

Move to Gransden, Bedfordshire, April 1943

10 in it - of different sections – the usual swearing type, so I am <u>as good as</u> alone in the hut. I got a good bed in the corner, with new biscuits and blankets and have installed myself. Our section is not yet organised - but equipment keeps arriving - and a hut has to be fitted up with equipment on tables as it would be in an aircraft. Up to now we've been painting the tables. Apparently when the scheme is started the hut will be used to train navigators and our work will be to service the equipment and that on the aircraft they use. This will be a change for me – it means working on the old 'fruit machines' and intercomm sets, which I have not seen since Bolton days. I said I felt cheerful – I don't feel really happy because I am lonely – but I keep persuading myself I must be patient and when more people come, I shall perhaps find a pal and have someone to talk to. Now about facilities etc. - you can get a wash in a hut next to us, but it is only cold water. Near the cookhouse is a big place with lots of hot water and some showers. Also near the cookhouse is the NAAFI - in which is a canteen, a sitting room and a wireless and newspapers. Unfortunately you cannot buy a newspaper here and must go to the NAAFI to hear any news. The nearest village – Great Gransden - is a very picturesque place and I have found the P.O. and a telephone box (cheers!) - when can I ring you - and I think I will go to church tomorrow night. The country is lovely and the weather very hot – I <u>have</u> got a red face! Through our officer I have <u>for the time being</u> got a bicycle (RAF type) and am saving my legs now. I am sure I am going to be happy and settle down soon, because my work promises to be so interesting under such a good officer."

Move to Gransden, Bedfordshire, April 1943

The hours of work sound very civilised between 9.0 am and 4.15 p.m and within a few days the Flight Sgt suggests that David should paint his name on the bike and appropriate it; "That is one of the advantages of being the first here", he comments. Some domestic duties are similar to before, but there is no cooking. Monday nights are devoted to polishing floors and windows. Quite quickly he moves from Hut 25 to Hut 26 – "in this hut we are all wireless mechs and will all be working together. Up to now there are 2 corporals, both very nice fellows, who are friendly and do not swear. I have continued painting etc., nailing oilcloth to tables and polishing it and tomorrow we are to start some wiring up. I want to get on the Stirlings and Lancs when they come and get bags of experience and swot for my LAC. There seems much more chance of progress than in the vicious circle that existed at Duxford Signals HQ. There should be some good chances on this new unit."

He travels by lorry to Oakington to get some supplies and is impressed by all he sees "You would be heartened to see the scores of monster bombers I see nowadays. It is a great experience to get into Bomber Command and learn the spirit there and compare it to Fighter Command. All the personnel are in barrack blocks centrally heated and there is a grand atmosphere pervading the camp."

Jock (the corporal) and David are put on Daily Inspection duties which means clambering about all over the planes and seeing to the wireless equipment "I would rather work on aircraft than be in the workshops all day, just fault finding and repairing. I expect it will

Move to Gransden, Bedfordshire, April 1943

seem a bit more nerve wracking when you first sign a form 700 saying the wireless is OK for taking up, but then at Babraham receivers the responsibility seemed awful for a day or two and then you got into the way of it." He seems to be incentivised by having work which is more responsible.

The downside of Gransden is the lack of news "The thing I miss mostly here is newspapers – the NAAFI buys 3 for about 900 fellows and you can guess how soon these disappear from the canteen. I usually hear a news bulletin once a day, the 1.0p.m. or 9.0p.m. I find on 3 days a week there is a Library." Unfortunately the village phone box has a very faint line, so communication is difficult all round. Eileen writes "get your best Town Crier voice on and I'll take my gas mask off and let's hope it will be 'loud and clear'." As regards the lack of newspapers Mutti "has partly solved the problem – she will send you some together with the Advertiser and Picture Post. Mutti says would you like the Sunday Chronicle as well?"

Eventually he manages to break out of the isolated camp with Jock and Eric (the 2 corporals) and they travel to Bedford on what the RAF call the 'Liberty Bus'. "It is a 35 mile round trip there and back and cost us 6d return! I _was_ surprised at Bedford – I expected a Sheffield type of town, but the shopping centre is very like Cambridge. There is a broad river flowing through the centre of the town and I noticed people rowing on it. We went to a nice restaurant and had some supper and how nice it was just to sit at a table, with cloth, - be waited on – watch people going to and fro - and take

Move to Gransden, Bedfordshire, April 1943

your time over your food." They go to the pictures and then search for a canteen. "An American Sgt told us the only place open was the 'American Red Cross' and said we could go there if we went as his guests – he took us in and insisted on buying coffee and cakes all round – he was a very nice fellow."

The camp settles down into a steady routine. Monday nights are not only 'domestic evening' for cleaning, but also can include a general medical inspection by the M.O (looking for infectious diseases such as measles) and a film show.

> "The show was all free and lasted 2 hours and was, indeed, great relaxation. First there was a Popeye film, then a newsreel – quite a lengthy one - and the main picture was 'Sun valley Serenade'. Sometimes there is a Duty Party from 5-7 p.m. It amounts to being available in the hut for these 2 hours in case there should be any transports to load or unload. You may have to go down to Gamlingay and load up lorries with bombs and then unload them here – that is just a typical job, but it is not very often you are called out for any jobs. Another duty is Aircraft Guard - my turn will be coming along – you take your blankets and sleep in the aircraft, just to ensure no-one runs away with it! That is only one night every so often."

Occasionally, too, he has to do a general guard duty of 2 hrs on 6hrs off, 1½ hrs on and then 4½ hrs off walking up and down the HQ offices on the drome, with rifle, bayonet, respirator, gas cape and tin hat. "I haven't done a guard since I was at Blackpool. The off duty 6 hrs means

Move to Gransden, Bedfordshire, April 1943

sleeping in the guard room, but you may not remove any clothes or boots incase the guard is called out. In reality it proves impossible to sleep because of all the comings and goings, aircraft revving up and other men snoring."

No passes for leave have been organised and David is wondering where he could travel to in order to meet up with Eileen, as there seem to be no public transport links. He enjoys a cycle ride to St Neots in May and begins to think that Peterborough might be the best place for a rendez-vous as it is on the main line. "All the 8 trains or so each day to Louth go through St Neots and don't stop!"

Wings for Victory week is coming up on 8th May and a variety of fundraising activities are being organised in Louth "They are going to have a rubber dinghy in the static water tank at the Market Place, for people to throw money into, they hope to sink it. We advised Mr Pitt, the organiser, to throw himself into it and sink it at one go." Eileen is in a generally jokey mood, it seems. She writes "We had a true comedy at the office the other day, when a woman came and explained that she had placed her tax repayment claim cheque in her basket, then had put dog biscuits on top of it; she went into the garden when she arrived home and left the basket on the path. Of course the dog ate biscuits and Repayment Claim; now she is trying to urge us to get her a new cheque in time for Victory week." In the same letter she recounts "Yesterday Mutti made a cherry tart for lunch and we did have a chewing competition, it was funny, I got 64 stones by the time I cleared the platter. Today I could only tackle 30 because I wanted to hurry and write your letter." She seems to put these little descriptions in to cheer David up and to keep him in touch with office life.

Victory Week turns out to be a victory for both of them, in that somehow David does get to Louth for a very short time. It is 5 months since they met but frequent letters have passed between them during this time, so they are very much in tune with one another. David still finds her a bit shy, but prefers her to be this way rather than "blasé and far too free with the fellows." They go to the Victory dance together and then he has to return to camp.

The weather is quite hot and he describes a Sunday afternoon spent trying to change an aerial on a Stirling "The metal of the kite was so hot we couldn't touch it with our hands. We had to remove the whole aerial running from head to tail and fix in another - then with a T-joint run another aerial down to the side of the kite. It sounds easy, but try walking on the top of a slippery fuselage from one end to the other – some 12-14 ft from the ground – unrolling wire from a reel. You must have no kinks or twists in it and when fixed, it must not sag. Then when doing the T joint in such a precarious position, it is not easy." The whole afternoon sounds full of potential mishaps:

> "1) I sit astride the fuselage and split my pants about 7" along the seam. This happened early on in the afternoon, worse luck.
>
> 2) A plane caught fire on the ground and we watched the fire engines tearing round the perimeter to put it out.

Move to Gransden, Bedfordshire, April 1943

> 3) This was just over when a plane came over with one of its engines stopped – looking as if it would land - it got lower and lower coming straight for us and we prepared to evacuate, when it picked up and rose above us.
>
> 4) A plane, going back to its place on the field, turned near us and had us in its slipstream - and we had to cling on or be blown off!"

The war is increasing in its intensity and there seem to be many more planes in evidence now. The Dambuster raid takes place around this time and Eileen writes: "Wasn't the Lancasters raid on the two dams a marvellous achievement, to think that 19 bombers could cause all that havoc and bring about more devastation than many big raids on the Ruhr; it's ironical too that it was suggested by a Jew." Closer to home she describes "Last Friday and Saturday we saw about two hundred Fortresses go over here, it was a grand sight, some of us went onto the flat roof of the office to watch them, they had such a mighty hum and their force and power seemed so encouraging." To some extent the war must have seemed a bit like a 'spectator sport' for those who had not entered the armed forces. Perhaps it was with this in mind that Eileen still feels she is not contributing enough to the War Effort. She now hits on another idea which partially remedies this feeling "Today we've had a circular at the office, asking for volunteers to go harvesting; apparently the Board will grant us a few days special leave if we will go to help with the sugar beet and potato lifting in the Holland Division, somewhere near Boston. I think it's a good idea because the farmers

Move to Gransden, Bedfordshire, April 1943

will certainly need some outside help if all the crops are to be harvested - at this particular camp they are planning to have 30 civil servants a week. I want to go if possible and some of the other girls and Mr Brailsford are considering it."

Girls of Eileen's age were coming into their own. New careers for girls were also developing. David recounts how his sister, Mary, now aged 19, has gone to train at a newly opened Domestic Science College in Leicester. He manages a trip by train to visit her in June 1943 after she has been at the college for two terms. His descriptions of the college are full of praise. "The kitchens and laundries are marvellous - plenty of equipment of all types - and their dining hall is wonderful. I saw the library and the cosy common room. All the furnishings, carpets, flowers in vases etc. are all so carefully chosen." He is able to take her for a Wings for Victory Dance at the De Montfort Hall and comments "It did seem strange to take Mary out to cafes and dances – and to me it seems incredible that she has grown up."

But he has also grown up quite a bit since he was last in Leicester and he is able to realise this by seeing other young men who are about to go through the same training as he had done "I saw a squad of airmen waiting about to be drilled – just in the same place and the same way as we used to. I saw airman in the workshops – visible from the road - learning how to solder and twist wires etc." Everyone is maturing and the war is possibly making them mature a little faster than they would

Move to Gransden, Bedfordshire, April 1943

have done otherwise. David is learning how to handle difficult people better. He writes "The sarcastic fellow is even pleasant these days. I have found by countering his sarcasm with my own leg-pulling sarcasm, the result is humour and a laugh."

He is now seriously thinking about his and Eileen's long term future together and gets on to the subject of marriage in one of his Spring letters. He quotes from some ideas which he has read "Marriage is rather like a book – a long book with many chapters. Physical love is one of these chapters – an enthralling chapter, but inconclusive and meaningless taken out of its context.

There are many other chapters in the book of marriage – companionship, understanding, mental stimulation, loyalty, the peace of loving each other so well that words are unnecessary, the skill of living happily together, the creation of family life, the practical economies of life." He asks Eileen what she thinks of all this and so begins a dialogue which leads towards them eventually becoming formally engaged.

For the time being, though, the duty of the war is the overriding consideration. David writes on a cold, wet day in June: "It was so windy and cold and Jock and I kept relieving one another, as our hands got too cold to work. Also we had to continuously replace the covers and retreat when the rain came down, then clamber out, slither about on the step, retreat again and so on. When I get cheesed, I remind myself that duty is duty and that's the end of it. I have come to recognise my duty more than ever before. In the Works Flight I would do the work, but thought much of a chance to dodge it – for any reason. At Babraham I got in a rut and nowadays am not sorry I left there, but here I am keyed up with interest - the 100% perfect kite as my daily object – and what is best about it – all this never strikes me as <u>work</u>, but as a great game which I am playing at, and yet getting paid for having a life in the country too. The game is never a drudge either."

Interestingly, though, long hard duties can sometimes lead to a lack of productivity. Eileen has routinely been doing 8 hours a week overtime as well as sleeping at the office on firewatching duty. It seems that the Civil Service realises that staff are getting worn down by the regime: "Head Office has, at last, come to the conclusion that long hours don't pay, so we are to put in 7 hours per week instead of 8 and are to have frequent breaks from it altogether." She writes that "it will be a joy to have more time to do things."

Light relief often comes in the shape of films, concerts or dances. David describes a concert "given by a Canadian troupe, and of course they received a great ovation from the Canadians here. At the end, each actor was introduced and his home town announced. There were loud cheers from various parts of the hall as different places and different states were called out. The chap sitting next to me was very excited. He was a Westerner and cheered loudly at each Westerner and kept telling me 'Oh, he's an Easterner'. At the end we all stood up and sang 'Oh Canada' and the National Anthem. These Canadians seem intensely patriotic and sang their national song very heartily. It is a great experience to live with a squadron of Dominion

Move to Gransden, Bedfordshire, April 1943

airmen." Eileen comments in response to this: "it makes you feel proud to see all these men from our Colonies here, living amiably with our men and fighting for our cause."

By mid-June there is talk of another move, but it is all hush hush and David does not divulge any details. The only thing he knows is that his 'A' Flight trio including Jock and Harry is likely to stay the same "We three are a grand team and wouldn't change Flights for anything."

12
Move to Warboys, Mid-June 1943

They do not move that far and land up in Huntingdonshire. "There are 9 of us - 3 corporals, 6 airmen and a Sergeant in charge and I can see we are going to be a good crowd and run our section all on our own. Our 2 Flight Sergeants are at Upwood, a camp some 6 miles away. Our life and our work here will be just as before and on the same kites. We are about 4 miles north of St Ives, off the main road, and about 16 miles from Peterborough. Now you can see why I need a bicycle. We are in a Nissen hut on Site 5 which is not fitted up with shelves, hooks etc. or electric light. It is awkward at present and we have been twisting pieces of wire to make hooks for our stuff. When this site is completed, there will be a big washplace and showers close at hand, but at the moment we must walk to the

Move to Warboys, Mid-June 1943

cookhouse site to wash etc." The RAF bike which he had been able to use at Gransden has not transferred with him and this now becomes his major preoccupation. He ponders whether to send for his own bike from Barnsley, but concludes that it is likely to go missing in transit, so starts looking for a secondhand one locally. Having toured around St. Ives, Huntingdon, Ramsay and Pondersbridge to all the possible shops, he could only find one secondhand bike and so snaps it up for £6-10-0. "It has been painted over, new tyres, new pedals a three speed and runs very well. I have already been offered £8.00 for it." Jock manages to buy a new bike from Pondersbridge, but it has no 3 speed gears. After these triumphs they cycle out to Pidley "and bought some strawberries which we soon ate. Then we went to Somersham and bought some lovely cherries and ate all those too! I bought a basket for anyone in the billet but by the time I got back, the basket was looking empty, so I kept it! Here end my adventures, covering some 25 miles by bus and hitching and 68 miles by cycle, all in 3 days!"

The ban on leave is eventually cancelled which means airmen can apply for day or 48 hour passes and even a proper week of leave. He has his sights set on taking 7th – 14th July and has worked out the best way to travel is to take the bike as far as Ramsay, then travel by bus to Peterborough from where he can get on the mainline train. Everything is looking up, including the camp food, which he compares with Gransden.

> "The outstanding features of the food today were
> 1) Milk on the porridge

Move to Warboys, Mid-June 1943

2) Extremely nice bacon
3) Soup as an extra for dinner is served each day
4) Coffee is available at dinner time
5) Plenty of jam.

No doubt these trivialities make you laugh, but to us they make all the difference between Warboys and Gransden. The billet has 11 men, all of whom seem to get on well together. The only slight problem is always needing someone to act as billet orderly to watch our stuff, as there are a lot of Irish labourers working round here, who think nothing of putting their head around the door on any excuse - to see whether damp is getting in or whether the electricity is in – and if no one were in, they would soon take a pair of boots or gum boots."

The work sounds more defined than before and David is enjoying the responsibility of it:

"I have been doing a 40 hour inspection on one of our kites. You see, when they've flown 40 hours, they go to the maintenance section for a 'glorified daily inspection'. As this was one of my own kites I was rather glad to be put on it, as I didn't want anyone else playing about with it. You have to do extra jobs such as greasing aerial winches, oiling generators with special oil, which means getting them out of their confined space under the W/Ops table. I have been lying on my back quite a time and all curled up too! Each job you do you initial on a sheet and the whole thing is very systematic. Another job is 'meggering the aerials' i.e. to see that there is no easy 'electrical path' between the aerial and the aircraft frame, which necessitates using a special meter. Tomorrow I am

Move to Warboys, Mid-June 1943

> going to start and overhaul a new kite, assist in the mods and eventually it will be my own."

Sometimes he has to sleep overnight in a plane. Even though it is June, he writes "10 am that's over and gosh it was cold. I had 4 blankets and even then was frozen. The dew was heavy and settles on the kite and all the metal inside becomes cold. It's rather like sleeping in an ice-box and at 7.0am this morning, it was far warmer outside!" He takes his duties seriously, but things do not always go to plan, however. He writes "Yesterday I had some excitement in a plane - I was near one of the large aircraft accumulators when it suddenly blew up and pieces of it hit my arm, luckily no acid splashed me, but the next thing was a trickle of acid through the floor through the bomb gear and eventually it streamed out of the bomb doors. What a panic of people rushing around with cloths, water etc. to wash it all away before any damage was done! The explosion as it went off was terrific!"

David seems to quite enjoy having something sensational to report which will mildly frighten Eileen. The next letter he writes in July finishes with "The Italian prisoner who shot the guard recently, escaped from near Upwood! And was captured and shot at St.Neots. Shades of Babraham Front Line. Cheerio my dear and lots of love"

Eileen's life is much more taken up with pleasant experiences and especially her work with the Brownies. In addition to her own group, she has started to help a friend who runs a pack of 30 children at Keddington. "On Saturday night" she recounts "we all went to a

Move to Warboys, Mid-June 1943

Garden fete held in the grounds of Birthorpe Manor; lots of children danced round a Maypole, it was a lovely olde-worlde scene, with the pretty garden, the bright ribbons of the Maypole and the childrens' costumes and the strains of 'Come lassies and lads' accompanying their steps." She is planning for a group of friends to visit, including David, and for them all to go on an outing to Skegness.

She writes "Won't it be spiffing providing everything works to plan? Of course, I know that anything might happen to prevent your coming, so I'm not counting on it too much." There have been quite a few cancelled day and weekend passes, so she could never be sure of him turning up. He does turn up and not only that, this seems to be the weekend in which he pops the question. On the Monday after he has returned to camp, she writes:

> "It is beautiful to anticipate the future together and now that we have decided, we can settle down to life with a true object. The past few months have been rather worrying and restless for both of us; sometimes I used to stay awake at night wondering what life would be in a few years' time. I knew that we had discussed all the essentials of a happy marriage, and I imagined how lovely it would be for us living together, looking after one another, sharing everything, having lovely holidays, and also in the less fortunate times when things went wrong, or we were ill, we should have the capacity to cheer one another up with comforting care and love; - all this I dreamed would happen one day, but sometimes it seemed so remote and far away, and I wished we could get over our young, inexperienced stage, and gain

Move to Warboys, Mid-June 1943

> enough confidence to plan for the realisation of our mutual longings. Now that time has come I have been thinking about the way in which we should discuss it with Daddy and Mummy and wonder if you think it would be best for me to explain why you are coming to them, when I get home on Friday night? For myself I think it would be less formal just to tell them and it would make it easier for you to talk to them. You would be able to tell your Father and Mother at the weekend too, if you wanted to."

David is overjoyed about everything and agrees with her approach. Both of them sense that their parents will be pleased with the news, as it seems the two families get on well together and respect one another. To add to his happiness, he is now put before a Board and made an A/C1 which means 9d a day more in pay! Not only that, but he has at last got his bicycle lamp to work. It was a standing joke in Louth that his lamp would never work properly for long. He now writes "You would laugh if you knew I had my bicycle lamp with me and have been applying my amazing electrical theory to it. I have discovered how it works! and it appears I never put the battery in <u>properly</u> before – consequently I earthed it and ran it down in no time at all. It's wired up wizard now and (technically!) has the bicycle frame as an earth return. This never occurred to me before when I used to use it." Life was looking up. His only fear was how long the war would go on before they could marry and where he might be sent to in the interim, "Churchill's speech was quite hopeful, what I read of it and accidentally picked up on the Marconi, but it looks as if we are all

Move to Warboys, Mid-June 1943

to be sent to Japan when this side is finished – so that means another 3 or 4 yrs in this blinking uniform, I expect!"

Nonetheless, everyone seems genuinely happy with the news of their engagement and David's mother writes a touching letter to Eileen saying "it has our sincerest approval and we trust this is also shared by your father and mother."

David has still got to formally ask Eileen's father on the Wednesday night when he visits, but he knows there will be "no upset or friction at all, and that they think that I am capable of looking after you." He seems a bit keyed up, despite this, and recounts two days beforehand "Nothing much has happened at camp today, except that I had another row with a nasty WAAF, who said I had already been round for one tea – and indeed I hadn't. She seems to dislike me, as she always puts less custard on my pudding and I always glare at her in return!" Perhaps his nerves were getting the better of him. He need not have feared. Eileen's parents had themselves gone through the experience of being engaged during the First World War. Their only counsel was to wait until the war was over to actually get married, but her father did say "he could safely leave it to our good judgement to decide."

When he gets back to camp, he finds that all the chaps in his billet have been moved out and the place taken over by 4 officers. He is now in a hut of 24 instrument repairers "who were happy and comfortable until we caused them to push their beds close together, took some of their hooks and so on and now they resent us.

Move to Warboys, Mid-June 1943

And as it's 24 to 5, we keep very quiet and aloof." They never seem to get any warning of moves which are afoot and one gets the impression that dromes were springing up all over East Anglia as the war intensified.

David is very much an airman who liked to keep his feet on the ground and know where he stood. This comes across in a letter written in August 1943:

> "Today Roy and Griff went up in a Stirling for a short trip – and wanted me to go – but not likely. It had been on the ground for weeks with something wrong with the undercarriage and fuselage, and it was only going on an air test too!
>
> In addition they went up in a terrific wind, with low clouds and rain - and without permission from the usual quarters – <u>and no parachutes!</u> It was all so irregular and risky that I wouldn't go. All the others were very surprised that they should have gone. Anyhow, they had a good trip around and saw St Ives and Cambridge from a new angle. Roy said it was very queer when they did a steep bank over St Ives. He looked to his left and could see nothing but the river and people looking up at them, and to his right was a wing towering for what seemed miles into the sky."

The overriding thought at the moment is the engagement ring. David receives a 'withdrawal authorisation' from the Post Office to agree to his taking money out of savings ready to purchase "something you will be proud to show to people and something worthy of yourself." Eileen is also thinking financially, but about what was known as the Marriage Gratuity. She tracks down the civil service regulations "In the event of

Move to Warboys, Mid-June 1943

marriage, a gratuity is payable, subject to a qualifying period of six years service. The amount is based on one month's pay for each complete year of established service. As a wartime arrangement, the Treasury will consider on their merits, applications for payment of gratuity where marriage takes place shortly before completion of 6 years service owing to the fact that the prospective husband <u>is leaving for service with the Armed Forces outside the United Kingdom</u>. It is proposed to work, in general, to a minimum of 5½ yrs." Thinking ahead in her imagination to the idea of a honeymoon, she comments "Oh dear it seems as though it will be Christmas 1944, it will be cold in Devon and Cornwall then."

Eileen is often a mixture of the practical and the imaginative. She realises she would have to give up her permanent job in the civil service once she does marry and she would not like to leave without her 'bounty', so it means carrying on as she is for the time being. But this does not stop her dreaming. She imagines a time when they will "go to nice dances again and we will have coffee in our own dining room in the firelight when we get home afterwards; it's lovely to dream all these things isn't it." Having coffee seems to be regarded as the height of sophistication, as far as she is concerned.

David is struggling again a bit with life in the billet. "The fellows are crude and talk a lot of emptiness, what they did last night, what women they are going out with tonight. I cannot imagine their wives would appreciate being talked of thus. I am sure these fellows are not in love with their wives and cannot respect them. I cannot bear to hear them revile marriage as they do, as I think

Move to Warboys, Mid-June 1943

it is something so pure and lovely, and I think about us and how lovely it will be when we are married." He is pleased to escape for the day to go and buy the ring with Eileen in Grimsby, but rather downbeat when he gets back to the hut, "The place has a somewhat gypsy air about it, as they are dirty looking fellows and one or two around me smell rather unpleasant. They make a lot of noise, shout, swear and of course play that confounded accordion hour after hour. We have protested strongly to our Sgt this morning and he is going to try and get us all together in a small hut." He seems to have been successful by September because he talks of having a "very comfortable billet now, with the lights in and a good bed, but illegal fire."

The couple manage a short weekend in Barnsley at the end of August when they are able to show off the ring and discuss future plans. David finds it hard to be as demonstrative as he would like to be when in his parents' home and has to explain this afterwards in a letter. "I am shy and have to wait till we are on our own. You can see how important it is to start our life together and away from our families where we are each entirely possessed by the other. That is the main reason I feel it would not be successful to get married in wartime and live at one or other of our parents' homes." His father encourages David to study for entry into the Executive grade of the Civil Service so that when the war does end, he is in a position to take the exam as soon as possible. David returns to Warboys vowing to study more during the autumn and winter months. The engagement is a great step forwards, but marriage still seems on a distant horizon.

Move to Warboys, Mid-June 1943

The war is making some progress. On 8th Sept Eileen writes "What wonderful news tonight, Italy out of the war, all the lives that have been saved, the great amount of time gained and the absolute freedom of passage through the Mediterranean and through Italy itself. We seem to have gained so many advantages now, while Germany keeps retreating all along the line in Russia, losing her only powerful ally; perhaps the end will be sooner than we ever hoped." David spends his 23rd birthday (11.9.43) doing guard duty, sorting out his kit and washing a muddy bicycle. Eileen spends the same day "bottling tomatoes and pears – part of my post-war planning!" Ordinary life must go on.

Mutti Lanc is delighted about their engagement and wants to make a tray cloth for Eileen's bottom drawer. "They scouted all around to find me a tray cloth to embroider, they are very scarce, but they did manage to get me one from a little shop near Steep Hill, Lincoln, so now we shall have to search round to find some silks to work it with. I do wish all these things weren't so difficult to get."

A lot of silk material had gone to be used in the making of parachutes, so it is ironic that in the same letter as she talks about the lack of silks, she also describes a parachutist landing in the garden of somebody living in Boston, Lincs. "They were telling me what great excitement there was at Mrs Martin's mother's house when a parachutist (one of ours) landed in her garden, his parachute was spread out all over the lawn, while the cords went right over the tool shed and he landed behind the shed. He wasn't injured at all, but he was

Move to Warboys, Mid-June 1943

very much shaken and was relieved when they readily opened the door and made him some hot drink etc."

Late September is dominated by the need to get the harvest in. Many women were encouraged to participate in this. David's sister, Mary, who has just finished her first year at Domestic Science college, has already done her duty earlier in the summer. She wrote to Eileen saying "On Saturday I am going fruit picking in Worcestershire with three of my friends from college. We are all obliged to a month's war work during the vacation and so we have chosen something which should be fairly pleasant." Less pleasant was potato picking which Eileen had volunteered for. "Everyone is giving me hints, suggesting that I take a pitchfork and prod 2 at a time, without having to stoop!"

She describes her farmwork experience as follows:-

> "Really Laddie I've had a lovely time working out of doors all day. I set off at eight o' clock in a bus from the village together with the rest of the gang. Joan, my cousin, was there and so I was able to be with her. Some of the women looked pretty tough and were dressed almost like scarecrows and some had curlers in their hair. When we arrived at the field at Rippingale, we were told we had to pick up the potatoes which had been unearthed when the soil was cross-harrowed; the original rows had been picked and these were the leftovers. We each got a basket and then lined up on the edge of the field, almost as if we were getting ready for a race and then we went across the 'breadth' as they call it picking up all the potatoes in the line of fire. Some of the women didn't work at all quickly because today apparently we were all to be paid 8/- and

Move to Warboys, Mid-June 1943

not on Piece Work rates, so they just ambled along, with the consequence that we reached the other side when they were only half way across, so we just sat on our baskets and waited for them - I liked that part, I thought of you leaning on your shovel in the Works Flight! After we had been there an hour, we had our lunch, we sat on the leeward side of the potato grave and had sandwiches and tea. We began again at 10 am and kept going backwards and forwards like a shuttle, resting at each end of the rows, of course, until one o'clock, when we again retired to our grave for dinner. This afternoon we started again in another field doing the same cross-harrowing work, but this time the field was on the slant and the horse which is supposed to follow us up with the cart, refused to walk uphill, it reared and bucked and we had quite a circus watching 2 labourers and an Italian prisoner trying to curb it. It kept tearing down the field as if it was going home; so finally as it was 3 o' clock the Ganger said we could all go over to the grave and wait for the bus. I'm sure I'm going to thoroughly enjoy this week. I was home by 4.00pm I've never known such times."

Although full of energy on the first day, by the end of the week she was not always picking up every potato, but sometimes pushing them back into the ground with her feet, so no-one would notice ! It was back-breaking work. She could have done with that pitchfork after all.

Even Mutti Lanc and her husband (both of whom must have been in their early 60s by this time) had had to undertake some farm work during the month of August. "They are both tanned with the sun, Mutti says she has been getting 'real tough' heaving sheaves of wheat up

Move to Warboys, Mid-June 1943

to Mr Forman on the cart; she also takes dinner and tea down on the bike to the men in the fields." It seems to have been a community effort to gather in the harvest and also to make the best of whatever natural resources one had to hand. Eileen writes "Mummy and I spent the day coping with two stones of Grimoldby damsons, we made 21 lbs of jam, bottled ordinarily seven 2 lb and pulp-bottled four jars full."

As a reward for all the hard work, Eileen treats herself to attending the Harvest Ball in Louth. She invites David and hopes that both he and his dance shoes will arrive in time. All the girls at the office are getting their long dresses ready and it promises to be an enjoyable event.

Dances seem to vary in quality a great deal and whereas this one proves to be enjoyable, many do not. David recounts his experience of going to a dance in Cambridge in October 43. He and a mate, Roy, suddenly hear there is a Liberty Bus from the camp to Cambridge and so change their plans for the evening. They go to a Corner House Grill first which is "full of officers and Oxford (or should one say Cambridge) accents. Our waitress was a nice fussy old dear, and when we asked for tea to go with a huge plate of omelette and chips, she said it was never done and brought beer in silver mugs! From here we went to a dance which was expensive and it was a lovely dance hall, with good lighting effects and a fine band. Unfortunately, the place was full of Americans and there was a lot of jitter-bugging. There seems to be a certain type of girl who goes to these dances purely for Americans. We found it almost impossible to get a dance, as most girls refused and next moment danced

Move to Warboys, Mid-June 1943

with Americans. In one quickstep a girl asked me if I jittered and said 'Oh, it's all the thing now' and appeared quite fed up. It is amusing to watch these women, whose whole purpose in life is to try to be a blasé American girl. They chew gum, and flaunt themselves before these fellows with all the glamour they can collect, and it's all so artificial. We left in disgust after an hour or two."

The weather in late October proves to be very foggy and wet, so this means that planes have to be grounded. There is really insufficient work for people to do during the day "The result of all this is that everyone has bags of surplus energy and everyone was so bright that they were running around in pyjamas tipping others out of bed. Pillows were flying around, but I succeeded in dressing without injury. Tonight I think I shall stay in and swot – do some Latin or German and waken up this slothful body!"

David's parents are due to celebrate their 25th wedding anniversary in early November and he manages to get leave to go home. His mother is so delighted she is nearly in tears to have all her family together. They celebrate with a wartime wedding cake made with "Australian butter my auntie sent some time ago." There are speeches and toasts and it makes David think ahead to how his wedding will be the next time they celebrate in this way.

In amongst all the frequent correspondence between David and Eileen are one or two copies of the *Inland Revenue Weekly Departmental Notes*. It seems that Eileen routinely sent these to David to keep him up to date with office regulations and developments. They look

Move to Warboys, Mid-June 1943

decidedly dry pieces of information written in small type on very poor-quality paper. However, I will quote a few excerpts from the Notes for 13th November 1943, as they give a flavour of the kind of austerity measures which had to be introduced to office life because of national shortages.

'<u>Sleeping bags for Fire guards</u>'. It is no longer possible to provide sheets for Fire Guards but a limited number of cotton sleeping bags may become available for purchase by individual Fire Guards. The cost of the bags is not yet known, but Fire Guards willing to buy them, if supplies permit, should hand their names to the officer in charge of the building, who should forward orders to the Director of Establishments A.R.P. Imperial Hotel, Llandudno. '<u>Fire Guard overalls</u>.' It is no longer possible to issue overalls to the Fire Guard, even on a duty basis. '<u>Supplies of adhesive plaster</u>' will not be issued to District Offices except in replacement of existing stocks, which have become exhausted or become unfit for use. '<u>Reinking of typewriter ribbons</u>.' It has been decided in view of the appreciable economy in material and manpower which tests undertaken by the Stationery office have disclosed, that used black record typewriter ribbons will in future be reinked and reissued.

Shortages of supplies are also evident on the RAF base. David writes "The weekly supply of coke comes about 2.0 pm. And is dumped about 200 yds away. Jock gave me this afternoon off and so I have been busy getting in a supply of coke. By 4.0 p.m. it will have gone because there is a regular procession of boxes, empty dustbins etc. I was there about 10 mins after it came,

Move to Warboys, Mid-June 1943

with a borrowed wheelbarrow from a civvy workman. After that job I set to work on my gum boots with a tyre repair outfit and patched one or two places where they have cracked."

Back at the farm in Billingborough there do not appear to be shortages. Eileen writes in November "I am going home on Saturday, Mummy tells me they have been fattening up a chicken for Sunday and she says I can make the stuffing, all the sauces etc." The week before that her father had been to South Somercotes to buy two bull calves. The only slight hint that they were being careful is when she sends David a cake in the post and says "I hope it will arrive all right. I made it this afternoon, but I'm afraid we hadn't any fruit to put in it this time as we are conserving our stocks for Christmas, however it is a rice cake, so I hope it will be OK."

Although there might be shortages in some areas, salaries seem to be rising. There have been previous awards of War Bonus rates and in November David comments "I see we have got yet another rise to 19/- per week now. Do we deserve it?" The way in which taxation was organized was also changing and Eileen writes "Everyone at the office is nearly tearing his hair trying to put the Pay As You Earn Scheme into operation, there are reams of instructions. Mr Riordan thought he would solve the problem yesterday when he got a rope off one of the parcels and said we could hang ourselves with it and save ourselves a lot of trouble." Presumably the country needed taxes for the war effort and PAYE was a quicker way of obtaining them rather than waiting for individuals to be assessed a year after they had earned their money.

Move to Warboys, Mid-June 1943

Some Inland revenue staff with families must have been finding it hard to afford Christmas gifts for their children because there is an announcement in the *Weekly Departmental Notes* dated 20th November which reads as follows. "The usual arrangements under which monthly paid staff in the lower salary scales may obtain an advance on account of salary due for the month of December will continue to apply. Eligibility for an advance is restricted to officers whose salary does not exceed £400. Normally the amount of any advance will not exceed £3." Presumably this was not an additional payment, but just the chance to have the money before rather than after Christmas.

David seems to have plenty of money as a single man and for Christmas he plans to buy Eileen an RAF brooch. The idea of this is to remind her in future years, he hopes, of the time when he was in the Forces and they had to manage a period of separation. He sends it by registered post, as they will not be seeing one another until after Christmas "I think the RAF brooch is lovely it's dainty and well-shaped and is just what I wanted; I have tried it on my costume lapel and on various dresses and it looks fine; it's nice to have it as a souvenir of this period of our lives, when we look back at it, we shall remember your being in the RAF, me being at the office, how we were both happy and how we looked forward for ages for leave and kept hoping for the end of the war."

A 10/- Postal Order mysteriously arrives for David in mid-December with a card "Best wishes from the Wellington Hotel." It turns out later that Mr Bowder

Move to Warboys, Mid-June 1943

at the Louth office belongs to some kind of club which has a Christmas fund for local boys serving in the Forces and so David has been nominated in his absence. In those days 10/- would have represented about 25% of his weekly earnings, so was no mean sum - 1943 was ending on a positive note. He was due to get about 10 days of leave at Christmas, which would allow for a main holiday at home followed by long weekend in Billingborough.

They have in fact managed to see quite a bit of one another over the Autumn since becoming engaged and both of them feel glad that he has not been posted overseas. Eileen reports that she has a new Inspector of Taxes and that she has been given Schedule D work, so she too feels optimistic about her prospects in the New Year. The tide of the war seems to be changing and with the opening up of a second front it is hoped that matters may be brought towards a speedy conclusion. Eileen writes "The meeting of 'The Big Three' sounds most promising we have just been listening to the combined declaration: let's hope when the Second Front does come into operation, it will move with such force that it overwhelms Germany quickly and so hastens the end which everyone strives for."

13
Still at Warboys, 1944

David writes a letter on New Year's Day "Last night's goodbye was also a goodbye to 1943 – for both of us a wonderful year, and to be remembered each year on 25th July. It is farewell to a year, but each future year holds more and more promise. 1944 has in store for us many meetings, planning and talking of our new life, and laying the ground for that happy day to come. Welcome to 1944!" His imagination has got to work as he envisages their future life together once peacetime has come. "You know, some aspect of the future will suddenly strike me and give me pleasant thoughts for hours. Last night it was of our future summer holidays and I fell asleep thinking of sandy beaches, sunshine, bathing, and at some date a small son crawling round his sandcastles in waders. And I could see his mother radiant in the sun, looking as young as ever and so happy." Eileen reciprocates these thoughts by commenting "I can often think of you helping our little boy with his homework, going to great pains to make it all clear to him, then when it's all done, having a game with him before he goes to bed." There is only ever a mention of having a boy, not a girl, so presumably this was a reflection of the general social expectations of the time.

As usual, David finds another welcoming family to link up with. It is a Baptist minister called Mr Kirby whom he is told about by a family friend and who lives reasonably close to Warboys in Bluntisham. Quite often he cycles over there and sits by their fire or goes for tea on a Sunday. They have a young daughter and sound to be very hospitable folk. They make his life more pleasant. It is often small pleasures that lift the spirits, especially during the winter months. On 12th January David writes "I had a lucky day yesterday – because when I went to meet the kites, the crew sometimes leave their rations of sweets etc. I found an orange! And some barley sugars and a packet of chewing gum. My morale went up in leaps and bounds – my whole day was coloured by the discovery of an orange – thus do little incidents please the mind in the RAF." Eileen realises how lucky they are to be able to meet up fortnightly at weekends, especially when she meets other people who have had their hopes shattered by the war. For example she encounters a young woman on the Grimsby train "she was a really lovely person, young and pretty and I felt so sorry for her because she told me that her husband, who was in the RAF, had had a crash and had lost one leg and injured his back badly, she had been to Rauceby Hospital near Sleaford to see him, she goes every weekend; all her story served to make me realise

Still at Warboys, 1944

how fortunate we two are, when so many young people are having to face so many troubles."

Often Eileen would extend the weekend visit from David by travelling with him down as far as Spalding and then returning by train to Louth. Quite how this was engineered is a little bit suspect, but it seems she did not always have a valid ticket. Whether she got on the platform by buying a Platform ticket and then boarded the train, returning to the same platform a couple of hours later is not clear. She writes "The train didn't get to Spalding till 10.20 p.m. and then all the carriages were in darkness. We groped our way in and found seats, we shared the rug and sandwiches and were very glad of them; there were 2 soldiers and a landgirl also in the carriage, so there was plenty of talking and joking about the slowness of the train, when I reached Mrs Lanc's it was quarter to one! Isn't it a terrible train? I was pleased the train was dark because no-one asked to see the tickets; 'men like darkness for their deeds are evil' it's me that is terrible now." David risked getting caught out by going back quite late. His train sometimes missed the 9.00 p.m. bus from Peterborough to Ramsey, in which case he then had to negotiate a night in the YMCA in Peterborough and catch the 6.55 a.m. bus back the next morning. From Ramsey he had to cycle into camp and made it by 8.00 a.m. just in time for duty.

Back at camp there is a defence training scheme. This consists of lectures on the semi-automatic Garron rifle, Sten machine gun, Browning machine gun and the Mills hand grenade. "Tomorrow morning we go in a lorry to Fenstanton, nr St Ives, where we each throw a real grenade! I've never done this before and hope there are no hitches or mistakes on anybody's part. I will write and tell you about it afterwards. On Fri we go to a range and fire the machine guns and on Sat we go somewhere else and fire the Garron rifle on a big range. I am not greatly adapted to guns etc. and shall really be glad when it is all over."

There is also rumour of a board coming up, so David plans to do a little revision in the hope of being made an LAC. In fact his Board comes up the very next day and he is called in for interview. "The Officer was an Electrical Officer who used to be a W/T Fl/Sgt and he asked me a lot of radio theory and had me drawing circuits of 'Leicester days' – all the stuff I had not revised!" As a result of this David is made an LAC as from 1st Feb 1944 and promises Eileen "next time you see me I shall have my 'props' on!"

As regards the hand grenades, he explains "We were given them in the lorry and had to take them all to pieces and clean them as they are greasy – when your turn came to throw, you went into a trench and fitted the detonator. It is a strange feeling when you pull out the pin and know that your fingers only are holding down the spring which would set off the whole thing and blow you up in 4 seconds. I threw mine OK and we all ducked in the trench. They go off with a terrific bang and you can hear pieces whistling over your head for a few seconds afterwards. Having now done it, I feel quite confident and would not mind throwing a dozen more. Tomorrow afternoon we fire the Sten and Browning. The latter is the same gun as in the gunner's turrets on the bombers."

Still at Warboys, 1944

Eileen teases him following this account "Don't bring any of your machine guns on leave – the razor, carving knife and toasting fork are quite bad enough" as it seems David used to terrorise people back home with these implements quite often!

If Eileen is becoming devious with her unauthorised train journeys, David is also becoming devious when it comes to obtaining unauthorised items. He writes "A registered parcel addressed to you will arrive in the next day or two – in which you will find two for you, two for Mutti and two for your mother. There will be no name and address inside the parcel and you will be able to disclaim all knowledge of where it is from – sounds like the dirty deeds of old, doesn't it?" Reading between the lines, these were precious stockings for the ladies. Had they been obtained on the black market? Eileen does not use the word 'stocking', merely saying "Mutti and I are very glad 'they' are on the way, we will pull their legs when they get here; I shall be going home on Saturday so I shall be able to take two of them with me and I'm sure they will be welcomed the other end; thank you very much indeed."

In a time of war, it seems as if people have to be resourceful if they are going to get through satisfactorily. For Christmas most of the presents were handmade items rather than bought and throughout the year there was an attempt to knit and sew various things or repair existing clothes. Eileen knits pairs of socks for her brother, Norman, and presumably this is why she wanted to obtain Class A/B wool. By February 1944 she is knitting a pair of slippers for her mother and she records "Mutti and I have been sewing the soles on, it has been quite a long performance, as each slipper has two thick felt soles and then a leather sole at the bottom and it's difficult to sew, especially round the toe part. However, we have finished them now and are quite pleased with the result, and we've saved 5 coupons." For Eileen's birthday her sister, Dulcie knits her a Cottage tea cosy and her brother makes her a calendar with a fretsaw.

Occasionally there is a glut of some food which they have been routinely managing without. David writes "We had 2 cookhouse surprises today – bacon and egg for breakfast and an orange for tea. In addition I got a pound of oranges at the NAAFI last week as part of the general issue to everyone."

When going to stay with someone for the weekend, it was important to send a ration card in advance, so that shopping could be done.

Obtaining books seems to have been particularly difficult. Eileen wanted a book on furnishing and hostessing and a collection of George Bernard Shaw's plays, but just had to join a waiting list for them. Sometimes it would mean buying secondhand instead. There are constant pleas from David to Eileen to send him back the used envelopes and writing paper seems to have been in short supply. Occasionally, though, quite posh blue notepaper is used bearing the RAF insignia 'Per ardva ad astra'. When it comes to birthday cards, David apologises "Sorry I could not get a birthday card – there were none in Warboys."

Someone special is due to visit the camp in February,

but they are not told who. It involves cleaning everything in sight "All these chaps have been messing about for a fortnight digging, sweeping, painting, polishing etc. One of our Halifaxes has had to be taken off flying, scrubbed down outside and in, all for inspection – what a game!" Later it emerges that the King is the dignitary due to visit and there are some positive spin offs for the men. "With the King coming tomorrow, the stores were very willing to change anything – the best mood to get them in! But what queues – I stood freezing from 10.15 a.m. - 11.20 a.m only to be turned away, as a lecture was on at 11.30 for everyone to go to. I went again at 2.30 p.m. and stood in the queue - wind and rain beating down, stamping about miserably and wondering if it was worth it, for nearly 2 hours. It was a successful affair as I came away with 1 shirt, 3 collars, a pair of pants, a tie, gloves, a pair of trousers, new PT shoes and a new pair of boots. How many coupons is that??!!"

More interesting from the historical perspective were the instructions given to the men on how to behave on the day: "Tomorrow's events are doubtful – we all have to go to work in best blue in the morning and line up and cheer somewhere after dinner. Officers are to shout 'Hurrah' with 'ah' as in 'far' and airmen are to shout with 'ah' as in 'hay' – that's an official pronouncement! One of our Halifaxes stinks of fresh paint, and has been cleaned down with petrol inside and out using 40 gallons! And Harry was telling me at one plane he was at, the hangar floors were cleaned of their grease with 2000 gallons of petrol to welcome the King! If only he knew how he was being deceived. He can surely never see the true state of affairs." Despite his scepticism about the whole event, David does seem to get caught up in the atmosphere: "They were due to leave the Mess at 2.15p.m. and we all lined the narrow road to give them a cheer - and here I had a really good view - they were in a car with big windows which drove slowly past and I was only 10 feet away. The King looked exactly like his photos in Air Force uniform, but sat straight up and looked straight ahead – he seemed like a waxwork figure to me, and his face looked as if it had suntan on it, as he had a bronzed and healthy appearance. The Queen looked lovely in her usual powder blue dress and smiling and waving. She looked just like her photos and very pleasant."

Following the King's visit, the ordinary work of the camp resumes and a miniature rifle range is installed: "We get 5 shots a penny – targets, binoculars and proper floodlighting – all to encourage the use of guns and aiming, I suppose, but it is good fun and jolly cheap at the price." For those that did not want the noise of the rifle range, to play snooker or to go to a film in the evening, a new Quiet Room was opened up by the YMCA. "It really is just what we have been needing on this camp. The room is neat, tidy and quiet. There are tables and chairs and neat little blotting pads nailed to the tables, easy chairs and a good big stove." Ideal conditions for letter writing! The padre took advantage of this new room to open up an informal discussion group once a week for an hour, when various general religious themes could be explored; "it was an entirely informal affair and we pulled our chairs around the stove, pipes were filled, clouds of smoke puffed up and this was the beginning."

Still at Warboys, 1944

Other evenings are spent doing guard duty, eating one's supper from a haybox and trying to keep warm in the guard room overnight. There seems to have been a lot of snow in 1944. Elaborate preparations are made for Eileen and David to meet up in March, when suddenly there is a setback. David has had an accident with his bike "I cycled round to see a plane back, and as always, when I got there, I lay my bike down on the ground near the plane. We all do this, as there is nowhere to stand them. When I got out of the plane, only 2 minutes later, I found the lorry which fetches the crew had driven over the front wheel and buckled it, and the forks beyond repair. I tried 3 shops. Only one promised to try and do something, as replacements are the trouble." He is not quite sure how he is going to get on leave, but comments "There are many chaps without bikes who go on leave just the same!" The problem of not having a bike is actually more acute on camp. "At dinnertime now I only have a few minutes spare, as walking takes up 45mins of my time. Gosh! I feel worn out when evening comes and can hardly feel my feet – and what is the worst indignity, people without cycles have to form up in groups of six or more and march from the drome to meals etc. Twice I have been stopped at the gate and have had to wait until there were 6 of us before we could set out." Luckily David manages to persuade his Flight Commander of the need for him to have a bike and a chit authorising this is signed fairly promptly. "When I look back on how I circumvented red tape, I am amazed at myself!" Thanks to the provision of a bike, he is able to organise a joint trip home to Barnsley in

Still at Warboys, 1944

March. He cycles 16 miles at night from Peterborough back to Warboys in record time, arriving back at 11.05 p.m. and "no effort required" because of the wind being right behind him.

For some reason he is moved from 'Flights' to 'Maintenance' at this point. "As regards actual work, it is more interesting – on the Flights there is no 'future' and it can become monotonous If a set goes wrong on the Flights, you just put a new one in and send the dud to Maintenance to put right. On maintenance you put your theory into practice and do much more practical work." The disadvantages of this change were:

> "1. You are not out in the sun and fresh air so much, but are stuck in the workshop and hangar inside a plane
> 2. I do not get so much freedom and cannot please myself as much as I did – it is not so easy to have an afternoon off or arrive at about 9.00 a.m. and have over 2 hours for dinner!!!
> 3. I have to work harder and longer hours on the whole – in 2 days I have worked about 22 hours"

He is pleased, however, that the Fl. Sgt trusts him enough to do this new work.

Meanwhile, back in Louth, Eileen is less pleased with the way her work situation is developing. She had been delighted when the new Inspector of Taxes put her on Schedule D work, as it gave her new experience and would perhaps have been a stepping stone to promotion to becoming a Tax Officer. Suddenly she is told that she is to be taken off this work "He explained it wasn't because I hadn't done the Schedule D work properly, he said he was pleased with my progress on that section, but he had had orders to put J.B. on it. I was staggered." Office politics were at work and J.B. was related personally to a senior person in the office. Eileen becomes quite indignant about it. "Isn't it the limit when temporaries get chances like this, through nothing but influence, and established people have to lose valuable experience as a consequence; it makes me so cross not only for my own sake but for yours, to think that if she gets through the training, she will be higher than the Executive Grade; I have no patience with such underhand, backdoor methods. I felt very cheesed off about it last week, but nothing can be done about it, so I have stopped worrying."

Thoughts are beginning to turn to post-war issues. Churchill gives a speech in which he outlines how the government will try to deal with the housing problem. David writes "The Government seem to be tackling it well and these prefabricated places are presumably just to tide people over the immediate post-war rush and are not to be permanent. The best piece of news in my opinion was that he does not think Japan will take so long after Germany. Last time he hinted it might be a long job. I wonder too how Bevin's demobilisation scheme works?" Eileen picks up on David's comments "Yes, I listened to Churchill's speech, it certainly was heartening to hear that there really will be a constructive policy about house planning, it wouldn't be too bad living in a prefabricated house – which has a certain amount of wall furniture - for one or two years, until there were some proper houses and nice furniture available. It would be interesting to know what the demobilisation plans are. I hope for our sake that they don't adopt a policy of 'First out first back'. I should think the 'key-men' question will be taken into account as well, though, shouldn't you? I think you will have to tell them that you would much rather do Income Tax."

David's view of their post-war life is very much a reflection of social attitudes towards married women which prevailed at the time. He comforts her in her work disappointment by saying: "These episodes will be forgotten someday. Your real place in the world is to be the darling little wife I know you're going to be and Taxes is only a temporary business – a means to a most delightful end – although it hurts to be treated as you have been and to have ambition thwarted." It is when reading comments like this that one realises how much attitudes have changed since the 1940s.

David's next letter is in a completely different vein. He is very much in the doghouse. "I am very sorry to tell you I cannot come tomorrow and I am very disappointed. I feel as if all the wind has been blown out of my sails, after making such elaborate plans and being <u>promised</u> a chit for Saturday morning from our Fl/ Sgt. It appears that on 14th March an order came out for everyone to go and sign for their blankets and pillow slip in a book. This had to be done by 18th March. I was on leave during this period and when I came back, I glanced through the sheets of orders and did not notice this one about blankets. When I went about my pass, he made me sign the book and said that people who had not signed it promptly were to have their next day pass stopped to

Still at Warboys, 1944

teach them to read orders. I have not a leg to stand on as there is no excuse for failing to read orders and you cannot plead ignorance on this account. On Sunday I have to report at 9.0 a.m. for general duties which might be anything from coal heaving to gardening. I feel so fed up darling and everyone agrees it is a very dirty trick. Please don't be too fed up with me will you dearest, although I deserve kicking, and I am very sorry too if Mutti has had a lot of trouble in preparing for me." He signs himself "Your most despondent, David."

Things improve the next weekend when he is able to get a pass to leave camp on Easter Saturday and meanwhile Eileen makes him a 'consolation cake' which is sent in the post, along with some chocolate and sweets from Mutti.

Eileen explains that she may not be there to receive him, as she has to work on the Saturday morning "We are getting heaps of people making enquiries about PAYE and the office has to be kept open on Saturday and Monday." The benefit is that she gets a whole day in lieu so is able to travel back on the Tuesday. This allows her and her sister and brother to plan the most magnificent 40 mile cycle ride on Easter Monday. "We found a sheltered clearing and made our fire (under an inverted bucket) and we soon had sausage, chips and eggs frizzling and we were ready for them after the ride. They tasted twice as good out of doors, inspite of being a bit speckled with wood ash! For a sweet we had stewed apple and custard out of our drinking mugs, which we had to wash, or rather clean with grass, before we could drink the tea we had brewed. Norman was in his element looking after the fire and Dulce and I enjoyed doing the camp cooking." In many ways Eileen comes across as more adventurous than David and more open to new experiences. When Bob, a mate of David's, asks if he will be best man at his wedding in May, David sounds a bit reluctant to get involved, but Eileen is all for going down to Staines and participating. "I am looking forward to it, I'm sure it will be a lovely weekend together, I like going to new places and I do hope it's nice weather so that we can go rowing on the Sunday morning too." She is often the one who encourages him to branch out more and she seems to give him confidence where he would otherwise be lacking.

For trips further afield there were sometimes restrictions placed on rail travel. By the end of April there was an order that no-one should go more than 25 miles on a day pass and this could not include the railway. Bob manages to get the requisite leave for his wedding and honeymoon, but it still hangs in the balance as to whether David will be able to get a pass or if he does, how far he will be allowed to travel.

There is no embargo on local trips and with the nice weather he goes down two evenings running to St. Ives and on the river. There he and Griff (a previous colleague) meet up and are negotiating a bend in the river when they meet another chap they know. They tied one boat to another which then enabled one person "to lie back like some Lord Muck in the second boat and sunbathe." Two hours of boating is followed by a good meal at the YMCA and then a pleasant cycle ride back to camp. People seem determined to enjoy themselves

Still at Warboys, 1944

whenever they can. Eileen gives details of a Parish tea, as if it were a great excitement. "It was really marvellous how many refreshments we managed to collect by each person contributing his share; there were sandwiches, rolls filled with egg and cress, plum loaf, home-made scones and heaps of varieties of cakes. It was the first Parish Tea since the beginning of war, as they have never dared to even attempt one in the last 3 years. Mr West sat near me and as he had come late, he hadn't finished his tea by the time we had and I couldn't help laughing when the Vicar announced he was about to say Grace, I heard Mr West say under his breath 'Good God I shall have to stop now!' We had a concert afterwards given by the Junior British Legion party, the children did very well with their dancing, singing and acrobatics."

As usual, Eileen is keen to take advantage of any opportunities going. She has seen details of a week's farming camp at Buckden which is not all that far from Warboys It is not until 16th Sept "however with a stroke of luck you might still be at Warboys, and in any case I should be able to visit Huntingdon, St.Ives and probably Cambridge while I was there and it would all be new ground." Although the other girls in the office are not keen to go, she is prepared to be the only applicant and she obviously hopes she will be able to see David in the evenings after work. Punting at Hemingford Abbotts would be a distinct possibility. "When you come to Buckden we must certainly go there. It is only about 6 miles away!"

Bob's wedding is getting nearer and they are both taken up with making the necessary arrangements.

Still at Warboys, 1944

Questions of a suitable wedding present are solved by Eileen touring the shops for either a set of carvers at 26/- or a set of teaspoons for 16/-. They plump for the latter because of the expense of travelling down to Staines. There are no such things as wedding lists. People just give what they can afford and hope the present is not duplicated by somebody else. Eileen has been quietly collecting a few engagement presents of her own as the months go by and these constitute her 'bottom drawer'. "Last night when I got home, I found a parcel from Mrs Turney waiting for me, when I opened it, I saw it was the tray cloth which she has been embroidering for me, it's simply lovely and is made out of some of my Irish linen, it is dinner wagon size, so I want to get two more exactly the same to make a set – all we want now is the dinner wagon!"

David does not relish doing a formal speech at the wedding and in fact has been suffering from laryngitis for several weeks beforehand. He reports daily to the M.O. for his throat to be painted with something and continues to gargle. Mr Kirby, the Baptist minister whom he knows, gives him quite a few pointers as to the duties of a best man and reassures him that a full speech is not necessary. With Eileen at his side he performs quite well "It was grand of you to come darling as it made all the difference to the whole thing, particularly so at the wedding where I felt much happier having a kindred soul there – I am sure you played a big part in boosting up my confidence. Wasn't it fun rushing round London and seeing all the famous places? It was like an adventure – indeed it is the first time we have ever 'gone places in

Still at Warboys, 1944

a big way', isn't it?" These experiences were obviously making quite a big impression on David because he says he has written 14 pages home to his parents about the weekend away!

Whilst down in the London area they had also linked up with one of Eileen's aunts (Ethel). It is amusing to note that following this David sends her 2 soap coupons as a form of thank you present for her hospitality.

The poor old bridegroom later gets into trouble with the RAF because of a mix-up about his leave. "Bob came back on Friday night, returning with Joyce. Apparently he was only given 6 days' leave, although she had 7, but he never checked his pass. He was on a charge, of course, and was tried yesterday by the C.O - 1 day's pay stopped and 7 days confined to camp He has to report to the Guard Room at 6.30a.m, 1.0p.m., 6.0p.m., 8.0 p.m., 9.0p.m, 10p.m. and between 6 and 8 he does fatigues. It seems a poor return to camp, but he says it was worth it. His advice to me is to get married without delay. So what do you think of that??!!"

Bob getting married seems to have had an unsettling effect on David "a very disturbing influence, perhaps you could call it enviousness of Bob and his honeymoon and I wished that I were he and that we were so fortunate - thoughts which led to the endlessness of the war etc. etc. The result was a desperateness." In response to this he engineers an unannounced visit home to his parents and this seems to restore his equilibrium. By the time he arrives at Peterborough to cycle back to camp, he sounds a lot more upbeat "it was a grand evening with sweet scents of hay and hawthorn briar in the still air, and I felt quite bright and called out 'Goodnight' to everyone on the road." Eileen appreciates the sentiments expressed. She too gets 'cheesed' sometimes "and I wonder whenever life will become settled once more and when we can definitely fix upon one place to live in and build up our home and centre our lives upon it, instead of living practically three different lives of 'Air Force and Office', 'Leaves together' and ' Going to our homes' perhaps it won't be so long now darling."

With talk of a Second Front starting imminently, no-one could be sure what would happen next. Troops were amassing and the Americans were very much in evidence. At Whitsun Eileen writes "On Monday afternoon I went with the rest of the village to watch the Americans playing Base Ball, it was really amusing because none of the spectators knew the rules of the game and so they didn't cheer at all and the players did all the shouting themselves; in fact they made an awful noise during the whole game, especially when they contested the decision of the referee, they used to yell 'G'an (go on) you're kiddin'." Playing sports must have taken their minds off what they were about to face. In fact D Day was only one week away.

On 5th June Eileen is very involved in a Brownie and Guide Rally, at which Lady Baden-Powell is to be the guest of honour. "Lady BP is quite tall, rather fat, and with a round jovial face, her voice is somewhat like a man's and she has a tough manner, very sporty, and yet so motherly, especially to the Brownies. She came round and shook hands with all the leaders and talked to lots of the children, including 4 of our Brownies."

Still at Warboys, 1944

D Day is declared on June 6th and Eileen writes "I have been wondering all day how the news has affected you, I felt a mixture of relief, excitement and fear for the men taking part; it has been most interesting hearing all the Observers' reports and I've been rushing home all day to hear the news." David writes "So at last it has come to us – rather unexpectedly I thought, although long anticipated – but how great it was to hear the first bare reports and rumours at 8.0 a.m. and by 1.0 p.m. the news rose to a crescendo as we knew what was upon us. It is a great day, darling, I feel it is such a great and awe – inspiring day that I hardly know what to write, although I feel I must write. It is as if a great tension has been relaxed and now there is no more waiting, but only grim determination in this final knock-out blow which is going to end the war for us all and bring us home to each other. It must be thus that millions of people feel and they welcome this, terrible as it is. They are very brave men who have set out today and I feel we should all think often about them and pray for their safety as far as is possible. I have felt my mere war effort so futile today against all this – life has been so much the same – detailed for site cleaning, NAAFI queues and cakes, same hours and same work, that it has been difficult to reconcile the great events with life here. I feel some regret at not being right in it, but should be scared I know if I were. Perhaps I shall get some satisfaction in a more active job later. Life here has assumed a more serious character and security is playing an important part. We shall have various duties etc. about which I cannot tell you, but we must always be in a state of preparedness, so

Still at Warboys, 1944

if any delay occurs between my letters, don't worry – I shall have been busy and have had no time to write. I have just been listening to the King and the news and all the eye witness accounts of the BBC reporters – I expect you are listening too. It is all very good and gives reason for confidence, although Churchill says the worst is to come. The initial landings seem to have been effected according to plan which is heartening".

Two days later he comments in a slightly guilty sounding way "It seems so irritating to be doing my usual steady job and not to be part of the greatest event in world's history. When 'they' say 'And what did you do Daddy in all this?' - what can I say?" Eileen also seems to be experiencing a sense of unreality "one feels it would be more realistic if one could go to the coast and actually see the ships taking part; when listening to the wireless it's almost like past rather than present day history."

The strange dissociation of it is summed up in a letter dated 11th June, "All this Second Front seems so unreal here in England and difficult to imagine it is going on at all, especially when you listen to a cricket commentary from Lords, as I did yesterday. No wonder the Germans think we are mad! I have been often reminded of Folkingham drome and of all the healthy young paratroops who were strolling in Bourne High Street as we were waiting for the bus last Sunday – I can't help wondering what is happening to them all and how far Bourne must seem from them They deserve such a welcome home when this is over."

Perhaps cricket is a stress reliever. In mid-June Eileen goes down to Mablethorpe with 2 friends to go around

Still at Warboys, 1944

the shops and then down to the beach. Once there, they encounter some soldiers who seem to be at a loose end "After a little while they asked us whether we would like to join them in a game of cricket. We thought it would be good fun, so they scouted round and found a piece of driftwood for a bat and piled clothes up to make the wicket and we had a fine game. The boys were really very nice and sporty, so we felt pleased we had played with them, there isn't really very much for them to do down there and they seemed to be glad that we were friendly towards them." Simple distractions such as these would perhaps take their minds off the thought that they could at any time be sent overseas to fight.

The closest David comes to any 'battle' is when 3 of them take a punt from Hemingford and then encounter a boatload of 'instrument bashers' from the camp. They give chase over a stretch of 2 miles ramming, mixing up their oars, pinching the rudder and beaching the boat in some slime and tall rushes. It obviously gives everyone a chance to let off steam and test their strength against one another, but of course it is only 'playing at war' and no more than hijinks typical of young men anywhere in the world.

The real effects of war are brought home to David when he has a letter from his old friend, Edgar, in early July. "He has arrived back in England, has had 14 days leave at home and is now in a hospital near Gloucester, having treatment for his rheumatism. He sounds to be very tired and war weary and to have little interest in the RAF or radio, but is glad to be back. When he is better, he expects to be posted to some station." Similarly

Still at Warboys, 1944

David recounts "Yesterday I met a wireless corporal who was an instructor at Leicester. I recognised him quickly and he said he had seen me before somewhere. He had an accident with a bomb and lost an eye and messed one side of his face up, but it was from his good side that I recognised him." Such sobering accounts are interspersed between lighter topics, but David is always conscious that he could be called overseas himself to an active theatre of war.

During the war most people did not go on holiday in the summer. As a result of the beaches being barricaded, there was not much to attract visitors. Many of the pre-war landladies who used to take guests had given up doing anything and so it seems surprising that Eileen's family is contemplating a holiday at Sutton-on-Sea, where they always used to go in the past. Eileen writes "Mummy, as you know, wanted us to spend our holiday at Liverpool, but really it seems hopeless attempting to travel all that way when the trains are all so crowded and needed for troops and for evacuating people from the bombed areas, so we decided that a more restful time by the sea would be much easier and would do us heaps more good. So first of all I went to Mrs Coupelands, the person we stayed with before, but unfortunately she couldn't accommodate us this time, but she gave me lots of addresses and I set out and tried them all. I tramped around for two hours with no success, everywhere was booked up and lots of people said they had been booked since January." She has a bathe, tries most of the houses down Trusthorpe Road and eventually returns to Mrs Coupelands' neighbour. "Mrs Barton had said that she

Still at Warboys, 1944

wasn't booked up because she didn't intend to take any visitors until after the War. I explained the position and in fact talked to her for about an hour and felt I had more or less persuaded her to let us go there. She said she would write and let me know her final decision so I had to leave it at that and run and catch my train home at 8 o' clock". The research paid off and the family would be able to get a holiday break from 5th August for two whole weeks. The beach was open in part for bathing and Eileen hoped to take a 10 day break from the office. David would be welcome to join them if he could get any time off.

His duties had expanded to include covering the stores because a mate, Brad, had broken his thumb in a cricket match and was detained in Ely hospital. Nonetheless, he does seem to get leaves and passes quite regularly. His sisters are down working on a farm in East Anglia as part of their national service and he is able to get to meet them at Billingborough in July which pleases him no end.

However, he is not able to get to the coast and misses out on some really good holiday weather. The closest he gets to enjoying himself is when he and another chap go down to Hemingford on the river. "We stripped down to our trousers and punted up and down, sunbathing. There seems to be an atmosphere of careless abandon and freedom down there – lots of people are holidaying there in tents and river boats and there is lots of swimming. You just dress and undress whenever you feel like it and no-one bothers, as everyone is doing the same!" Eileen is more demure, she writes "It's marvellous here, we can just undress in the beach huts which have been damaged by high tides, we have found one which has seats and cupboards in it and have rescued pieces of doors and bits of wood and have patched it up with them. We have also improvised a net and can now play deck tennis on the sands. I have been doing some embroidery too."

While all this holidaying is going on, men are risking their lives on behalf of King and country. David writes "The news from France is fine – and I have just heard about rioting in Paris and a bridgehead over the Seine now. I think most of France will be in our hands by Sept 1st." Eileen comments on 24th August "Isn't the news marvellous? Paris and Marseilles liberated on the same day, really it's nothing short of a miracle the way that all our Forces are collaborating with the French troops of the interior and advancing rapidly in every sector. Everyone was staying up to get the midnight news, it was then that we heard the news of Rumania's peace terms with Russia. All this makes one feel very keyed up and apprehensive, watching history being made, don't you think so?"

Suddenly at the beginning of September there is talk of a 'fruit machine' course which David is put down for. "The course is held at Marconi Radio Works in Chelmsford with civilian lecturers and civilian billets. From all accounts it is a very good course and everyone who goes seems to have a super 'civvy' time." As it was only to be for 2 weeks, he would be back in time for when Eileen was due to start her farming week at Buckden. Plans seem to be working out this time.

On the European front there have been many

developments since D Day as Eileen writes on 3rd September. "This Sunday has been a most memorable day, hasn't it? The fifth anniversary of the war, and now at last the end is in sight, the Allied armies are driving through France and are tonight very near to the German border at Metz and Nancy and are also crossing the Belgian frontier, while the Russians are pressing in from the east and have forced Bulgaria, Romania and Finland to give in and cease to fight for Germany. At the National Day of Prayer at church today we were asked to cast our minds back to the days of 1940, and to compare our position then with our position now, and one felt that there had been a miracle to bring about such a change; and when in the prayers we heard 'Let the issues be decided in the cause of righteousness', one felt that we were going to be granted victory and to be trusted to use it to bring about a better, more Christian world. When I watched the faces of all the little Brownies, they seemed to bring home the meaning of the times more clearly to me than anything else, the children all looked so happy and well cared for and I realised how wonderful it will be when all the children in Europe can be free and contented as they are; and how everything must be done to avoid another war during their lives. I'm sure I shall always remember this day vividly".

14
Chelmsford, September 1944

David is detailed off to his wireless course at Chelmsford and is billeted with a Mr and Mrs Herson who have already had more than 400 airmen through their house in the course of the war. She sounds to be a homely type, judging by the fact that she had "the previous Xmas received 153 cards from either the airmen or their wives and mothers." The course is quite intensive and led by "some tip top teachers, brains of the Marconi Co, including the designer of the set we are studying."

Meanwhile Eileen is keen to ensure she definitely gets her farming week at Buckden. The boss does not really want to spare her from the office "he wants me to take great care not to work so hard at Buckden that I make myself ill and then have to have sick leave. I'm

Chelmsford, September 1944

looking forward to coming ever so much, in fact I must admit I'm rather like a child getting excited about a new adventure; it will all be a grand change from the office." She is busy painting her bike wheels black and getting it ready "for all our expeditions." By 12th September she reports "I have also some more good news, we haven't to do fire watching anymore, last night was the last night of duty." Presumably with changes in the fortune of war, the risk of bombing was not deemed to be great any longer.

Somehow David manages to get up to Barnsley for his birthday on 11th Sept but misses a train connection back to Chelmsford on the Sunday night. Luckily at Liverpool St. Stn "I met another fellow, who is on the course here and we discovered there was a mail and newspaper train to Clacton at 3.20 a.m. and that it was a hush-hush secret that one carriage is put on for Servicemen only – the stragglers' train. We got into it about midnight and slept on the seats until about 2.0 a.m. Then some soldiers arrived and we had to sit up and make room for them. Eventually, after what seemed an eternity, it was 3.20 am and we left. It was a very fast train and I don't think it was supposed to stop at Chelmsford because it slowed down and as we jumped out, it started up again. I was in bed by 4.30 a.m., but it very soon seemed to be morning."

15
Return to Warboys, September 14th

The potato harvesting week at Buckden is a great success and enables Eileen to meet up with David in the evenings. "Now I seem to know all the places near Warboys and am able to imagine exactly your life there, your friends and the way you spend your time. Last night I started to write a diary of my farming holiday and the account of the first Saturday and Sunday took two sides of foolscap paper! I thought it would be so nice to read of all the little incidents, although I know I shall never forget what a lovely time I had." The boss at the office was right – Eileen did catch a cold and he said "he wouldn't allow any of us to go farming next year, still I'm not worried because I've had my leave now."

With the advent of Autumn thoughts now turn to what opportunities there will be post-war once people are demobbed. David has had a reply from the Civil

Return to Warboys, September 14th

Service Association to say that "as I did not get Higher and did not receive full-time education up to at least 17, I am not eligible for the Open Reconstruction exams. I am, however, eligible for the Limited Executive Competition which is restricted to established Civil Servants. They say the Limited Competition will broadly correspond to the Reconstruction exam as regards subjects. That clears the air anyway and I shall go in for the Limited Exam." He sees the Executive Class as "the gateway to everything and I am convinced that it is worth every ounce of effort on my part to pass the first exam after the war. It will mean so much for both of us and I am going to try and do much more study."

Eileen is encouraged by this "You know, Laddie, it gives me such a lovely warm feeling when I hear you planning for the future and it makes me so proud of you when I know how eager you are to provide a good home and security: I'm just longing for the day when all our dreams and plans come true, it's certainly worth working and waiting for, isn't it?"

The nature of the war effort is changing. "Yesterday we had a very tiring day rushing around preparing a lot of our Lancs for going away (for good!). We still persist in good and bad rumours about leaving or staying, though when the bulk of our planes go, there will be nothing to do unless some more come!" By mid-October he comments "The nights are quite peaceful here and were when I was on leave." He is temporarily put on a different job "fitting up a system of intercommunication between the C.O's office, the Adjutant, and the Orderly Room. Each has a little box on the desk and leans over

Return to Warboys, September 14th

to speak into it, just like on the pictures in these New York offices! Any party can speak to any other party without the third one hearing."

Communication is generally opening up more. David receives a letter from his French penfriend - the first in 5 yrs. "He has spent some time in the Navy and now is with the French Army in Italy, having been at Cassino, Rome, Florence." It is possible to write to France now, according to the Post Office, but Belgium is not yet on the list. "The postage rates are 3d for the first ounce and 1½ d for each additional ounce." Eileen's penfriend lives in Lyons and David advises "Lyons was the FFI headquarters and must be well and truly liberated by now", so probably correspondence could resume.

The European situation might look more encouraging, but the war against Japan was by no means certain. The only slight reference to this comes in the shape of a pay rise backdated to 3.9.44. It is called 'Japanese campaign pay' and is 7/- per week extra for people with 3 yrs service and 10/6d after 4 years.

16
Course at Cranwell, November 1944

It is unclear what this short course was about. David was not impressed with Cranwell: "This place seems very desolate, no friends, no nuffinck, as yet" and he refers to himself as Convict 1080709.

The only redeeming feature is its proximity to Billingborough, which he manages to visit several times, meeting up with Eileen who is home on leave. Nonetheless, he gets 92% in the final exam before returning to Warboys.

17
Return to Warboys, late November 1944

By this stage thoughts are turning towards Christmas and New Year. Each is trying to plan what might be possible. Eileen is hopeful of getting 23rd December – January 4th which would enable her to travel to Liverpool, having missed it the previous year. David is less sure about what will be granted: "The official announcements of restrictions have not yet been made. There has been a preliminary announcement about the travel ban period and, also, that leave may not involve <u>outward</u> travel on a Saturday or Sunday. Whether this is to be rigidly enforced I do not know, but as things stand at the moment, I may have to travel up on Friday 29th Dec and return on Sunday 7th. I do not want to return on a Sunday as the travel is so awkward. Therefore I cannot just now tell you the exact dates." He seems a bit

Return to Warboys, late November 1944

Wireless mast. David is on the left of the front row.

preoccupied at this time and some of it is down to the fact that he has lost his comb!

Several letters refer to this: "I do hope you find my comb as I am in such a mess without it – or, if possible, can you get me a new one anywhere?" It sounds to be impossible to obtain a new one and Eileen promises to continue the search at home: "we will send it if we find it. Later she writes: "I managed to get you this one in town today, I'm afraid it's rather like a rainbow, but it's the only one in Louth, none of the other shops had any; don't let Bob see it or he will have some cryptic remark to make probably about waves in your comb, but not in your hair."

Finding items for Christmas gifts continues to be a problem. David writes "I do hope you are having success with the fountain pen, as I still want to get you this" -

Return to Warboys, late November 1944

she had first expressed interest in a fountain pen about 2 years previously! Even cards are not easy to find "I believe I must have purchased the <u>last</u> six Christmas cards in Barnsley and even they are not up to much."

Used envelopes are still being sent to and fro because of shortages so that they can be sent again to the same address. Household items are greatly treasured as presents "Yesterday I had a letter from your Pop telling me that he has managed to get an Electric Iron for Mummy, he is having it chromium-plated for her, she will be glad to get it."

By mid-December things are looking up a bit "I have got my leave application put in and tonight on clothing parade I have got a new suit of blue which fits very well, so I shall be able to look quite respectable at Liverpool." He experiences a slight setback when a

The radio mast at Warboys

Return to Warboys, late November 1944

Menu

SOUP

CREAM OF TOMATO

JOINTS

ROAST STUFFED TURKEY
& BREAD SAUCE
ROAST STUFFED PORK
& APPLE SAUCE
ROAST BEEF & HORSERADISH SAUCE

VEGETABLES

ROAST & CREAMED POTATOES
BRUSSELS SPROUTS PEAS
BRAISED PARSNIPS
CAULIFLOWER

SWEETS

CHRISTMAS PUDDING & RUM SAUCE
FRUIT JELLIES & CREAM
MINCE PIES
CHEESE & BISCUITS NUTS COFFEE
BEER MINERALS

CIGARETTES

Glasses are not available. Airmen will use their Service mugs.

piece of melted solder splashes up into his eye. This was in the days before any safety glasses. "When I recovered from the shock, Bob did a marvellous bit of first aid and whisked out the piece in one attempt. I discovered a very minute piece was embedded right in the middle

Return to Warboys, late November 1944

of the pupil, but could not feel it. I went to the M.O. and he deadened the eye with some cocaine and then told me to look straight at him. It was an extraordinary sensation to know he was wiping the eyeball with cotton wool and then with a pin-pointed instrument, he picked it out and I did not feel anything at all. It was painful when the cocaine effects wore off and I was unable to read, write or keep it open, so I went to bed about 7 pm and this morning it was perfectly normal."

Christmas itself is to be spent in camp followed by a New Year visit to Liverpool where David anticipates meeting all of Eileen's relatives again. A rather posh Menu and Entertainment programme card is given to each airman, on the front of which is written "Christmas 1944 The Commanding Officer and Officers Wish you all a Happy Christmas 'It's Nae Bother' RAF Station, Warboys. The idea, as usual, is that the officers serve the men this one day in the year. The menu is quite sumptuous.

As to the entertainment

    10.30 a.m. Soccer match: Officers vs Sergeants

    12.45 pm. Airmen's Christmas Dinner

    14.30 Impromptu concert and wassail followed by cinema film 'Forever and a Day'

    17.00- 20.30 Airmen's buffet Tea and Suppers

    19.30 Cinema film 'Forever and a Day'

Return to Warboys, late November 1944

> 20.00   Station Dance, fancy Dress (Gymnasium)
>
> NAAFI Institute will be open during the hours 10.00-11.30 and 18.00 -19.00
> Warboys Club 14.00 – 19.00 hrs

It sounds as if this was the best Christmas David had experienced since joining up. On Christmas Eve "the WAAFs were in a good mood and gave us some supper, after which we found all the chaps sitting around the stove in the billet singing carols and songs and we had a merry time till midnight. Then half played cards and Stan and I played darts until nearly 1.00 a.m."

On Christmas Day "Bob and I went to Communion at 7.30 a.m. and met Barbara there, so we invited her to breakfast with us – the WAAFs have their own mess, but no-one minded. At first there was a possibility of work and flying, had the weather been fine, but as ever it is foggy and the loudspeakers announced 'All personnel may stand down and <u>retire for revelry</u>!!!'"

Reflecting on it all on Boxing Day, David is obviously very pleased. "We had 2 officers waiting on a table for 10 of us, who autographed our cards. The mess looked lovely, everyone wearing paper hats – the band playing - and as we waited, we sang the tunes and everything was very entertaining.

Our Groupie came round to each table, dressed in a pinafore and Scots Glengarry, spoke to everyone, signed all our menu cards and had a drink at every table. Revelry certainly prevailed and everyone was very merry. I never ate so much in my life before!! and that

Return to Warboys, late November 1944

is saying something. I do recollect walking back to the billet with a handful of mince pies and pockets stuffed with nuts, oranges, apples and cigarettes and after a rest I set out for Bluntisham." Given that Eileen had also sent him a tuck-box as a Christmas present, he was well provided for and it is hard to believe that there was still strict rationing.

Eileen too had a good time with 14 relatives sitting round a table which had been expanded by placing a table tennis table over the existing one. "even then we hadn't much elbow room; there were lots of jokes, wise-cracks and plenty of laughing and fun." 1944 is finishing on a much more positive note than the previous one and hope is in the air that this next 12 months will be 'our year'.

18
Still at Warboys, 1945

Time spent with both families over the New Year period seems to have cemented the relationship even more and there is the hope of possibly getting married sometime during this year, preferably in July.

However, 1945 does not get off to a very good start, in that Eileen's mother is hospitalised with a duodenal ulcer and has to be put on a very strict milk diet when she eventually comes home. Eileen returns to Louth with a thick cold and David is complaining of muscular rheumatism in his neck! There is snow on the ground and he returns on a packed train where there is standing room only.

Reflecting on serious discussions which he has had with his parents over the New Year, he writes that they are sounding a cautionary note about his getting married before he is properly established in the Executive grade to which he aspires.

Still at Warboys, 1945

> "Father said he had high hopes that I would get my Executive so that we should have an assured position and good start – and that if I already had it now, he would not have the slightest hesitation in saying 'Yes'. On the other hand, I tried to point out that it was almost impossible to try and attain absolute security with things as they are in wartime – and that quite a time might elapse before I got demobilised and exams were again underway – unless one can take a reconstruction exam in the RAF immediately after Germany was defeated. I said I felt I could study just as well in a furnished flat or rooms of our own as I could in camp (or, after the war – in lodgings) and that you would be able to help me. Another point we discussed was whether we were prepared to accept all the responsibilities when married. They mentioned children and there perhaps being one whilst we were still in rooms or while there was plenty of study and worry as it was. And if there was, what arrangements would be made for you and here we reached the point where it was necessary to know what the viewpoints of your parents were."

There is quite a lot of deferring to the older generation, given that by now David is 24yrs old, but he has still set his heart on a July wedding, irrespective of wider world events.

He writes "It would be a wartime wedding and not quite as we had planned, with top hats and all the usual things which make it such a perfect day – but these are only small considerations." Eileen gives her considered reply in her next letter.

Still at Warboys, 1945

"Myself I do feel that we ought not to wait indefinitely, it does not seem sensible that when we love one another so much, we should have to live most of our life apart, just longing for leave when we can see each other; when one looks at life as a whole, every year seems so precious and during the war the years appear to slip by so quickly, that one feels that this, the very best of our life, when we are young and energetic and find such a joy in each other's companionship, should be spent together … if, of course, the war did go on for years and we did decide to have a child, I know that I could always live at home ... as to the question of a wartime wedding this, as you say, is of secondary importance, in any case I'm quite sure we could have a pretty wedding even now it would be a very happy day with the nice reception at home."

She sounds mature in her thinking – perhaps it was not coincidental that she was cutting a wisdom tooth around this time!

David does take to heart some of what his father has said because by 10th January he has sent for the Metropolitan College notes on General Knowledge which he would need to study for the Reconstruction exams. He has also asked Eileen to give him back all the Income Tax Instruction books so he can update on the procedures and regulations. However, he is also due to go on a wireless course at Farnborough and so explains that this will have to take precedence over any other studying.

19
Wireless Course at Farnborough, Hants 21st January 1945

He makes his way via Kings Cross where there is a loud explosion (usual sign of a rocket) to Waterloo, where he manages to get a train to Ash Vale and then walk. The Service Police are helpful and on arrival he is issued with a chit for a dinner by the Orderly Room. Very quickly he meets a Corporal whom he recognises from childhood. "We used to go to school together and play and quarrel at marbles!" Another man from Barnsley he recognises as having been in his father's church choir. Eileen has given David the address of her uncle Jack who lives in the area, so he is not short of contacts. The work is not easy "Our course is very hard and I suffer from brain fog by the end of the day and just have my

Wireless course at Farnborough, 21 January 1945

tea and dash out. I have not had to concentrate so much for a very long time and after an hour or two of lectures I feel almost saturated - we shall probably not <u>see</u> the set we are studying at all, as the course is on principles only – and if we do see it, it is certain we shall not <u>touch</u> it. We may not take any information out of the lecture room." Because of his rank, he has to march to lectures "I do feel soft marching with them all", he comments.

20
Return to Warboys, 29th January 1945

By the time he arrives back at Warboys he has nearly lost his voice and has to report to the M.O. He is put in the Sick Bay which he seems to quite enjoy; "I have spent the day in a cosy bed with sheets, looking out at the snow. I have to have various pills and gargles etc. but even being in bed is beneficial. Tomorrow I think I shall write to your mum – from one patient to another - it will amuse her!" Eileen's mother is eventually allowed out of Stamford Infirmary on 4th Feb and Eileen drives over to collect her in the Morris 8 belonging to her father because her father has hurt his shoulder. With both parents unwell, Dulcie is given a Doctor's certificate to stay away from school for a couple of weeks. Fortunately with them living on a dairy farm, the milk diet can easily be continued. All these medical complications mean that it is not really

Return to Warboys, 29 January 1945

opportune to mention wedding plans just yet, but David seems to think they have 'plenty of time' before July.

Eileen has seriously started looking at the Marriage Gratuity which she would receive on leaving the Civil Service as a permanent member of staff.

> "I'm glad War Bonus counts in the gratuity. I think I should get approximately
>
> £90 worked out like this Salary £2 : 11 : 0
>   Allowance   6:0
>   War Bonus   18:6
>
>   per week   £3 : 15 : 6
>   x 4
>
>   per month   £15 : 2 : 0
>   x 6 (yrs)
>
>   £90 : 12 : 0
>
> I'm just a bit worried Laddie to know what your reactions would be if I had to leave the office and go home to look after Mummy, the Doctor says she will need complete rest for a long time, if she overworks herself she is liable to have another attack and I can't let this happen on any account. I don't feel it is fair to Dulce to expect her to stay at home when she ought to be training for her career. I want to do all in my power to help Mummy and her life is more precious than any material thing, isn't it? I realise that if I had to adopt this course, it would confuse all our 'joint income' calculations, but I should live at home and should have to come to some arrangement with

Return to Warboys, 29 January 1945

> Daddy so that I could have my own money for clothes etc. and to keep my savings at their present level, I think he would be willing to compensate me in this way. I don't know whether you would still feel we could get married this summer, the trouble is that unless we get married within three months of my leaving the Service, I should lose all the Gratuity. Oh darling I'm so sorry to rake up all these problems when everything was working out so well. I feel it is my duty to go home, if I'm needed, and I couldn't bear to think that Mummy made herself ill again when I might have helped her and made her better to tell you the truth I do feel worried about all this and its effect on our plans."

With further medical enquiries, they find out that it is not just a duodenal ulcer, but that her mother is suffering from a weak heart, which is why she tires so easily. Given this, there is no question about what to do for the best. Dulcie is due to go to teacher training college in the September and Eileen would plan to leave the office in early July. If by any chance her mother improved dramatically and David were still in the Forces, Eileen would plan to get a job as an unqualified teacher. David is happy with this idea and they start firming up arrangements for a summer wedding. Eileen writes in late February

> "Yesterday I started putting our plans into operation in earnest – by making tentative enquiries about white material for a wedding dress. I went to all the shops, but couldn't find any I really liked, it seems to be very scarce, however I've found out

when they are getting their new stocks in and have also seen a pattern which I like very much, so I'm confident that I shall get one all right in the end; it's fortunate that we have plenty of time to make all these arrangements. Nan has offered to lend me her pink net bridesmaid's dress - the one she wore at Evie's wedding – it's very dainty and pretty. Margaret Rowbotham had one like it, so yesterday I went along to see if she would lend me it, unfortunately she had let it go out on appro to another girl, who is thinking of buying it; she says if this person doesn't buy it she will give me the chance to do so. I wasn't able to match the spotted net material here in Louth, so I will send the belt of the frock and perhaps your mother could see if any of the Barnsley shops have it. I'm also writing to some of the big London firms. By the way Mrs Rowbotham told me yesterday that she wants to sell Mr Rowbotham's morning suit, he only wore it at his daughter's wedding, so it's in perfect condition. I thought I would mention it just in case you would rather wear one than uniform. I think it would be about your size."

Only two days later she eagerly reports:

"I've just been on a most exciting mission – taking my white material to the dressmaker and arranging how I shall have my wedding dress made; and now I've settled down to write to you about the choice of a honeymoon spot; oh Laddie, all these preparations make me feel so radiantly happy. I certainly think North Devon seems a lovely part to go. I have looked up all the places you mentioned in your letter and have also read the two Guide Books which I am enclosing and

Return to Warboys, 29 January 1945

> the country and coastline seem ideal. Ilfracombe, with the exception of Lynmouth, is the only coastal place directly on the railway line."

One of her aunts, who was rather posh, had slightly put her off Ilfracombe, describing it as a 'trippery place', but said she "could highly recommend the Berkeley if we did want to stay actually in Ilfracombe." With the war being nearly over, pressure for holiday bookings was already building up and so there was a certain amount of urgency.

Next comes the question of photographs and how to obtain films. She quotes the sizes of camera as being Brownie No 2 i.e. 620, 120 or 20 film for Mr Pitt's camera and Brownie No 0 for hers. She hopes Mr Kirby with all his photographic connections may be able to obtain some films, which were also very scarce, it seems.

Despite this flurry of activity, Eileen has still not discussed with her parents the proposal for her to give up work and care for her mother. March has arrived and she plans to broach the subject carefully. David has already sounded out his Warrant Officer as to whether he can have 14 days leave for his honeymoon in July or whether he might be about to be posted elsewhere. It all sounds quite hopeful that he will be granted leave and that this would be honoured, even if he were posted.

It seems that Eileen's mother is "ever so glad to think that I would be willing to live at home afterwards" because up to this time she has been helped out by a succession of sisters, all of whom have their own commitments and live either in Liverool or London. Dulcie is no longer able to stay off school because she needs a good reference for Lincoln teacher training college, so all in all Eileen's suggestion is welcomed as a potential solution.

Excitement about buying items for the wedding day is palpable. Eileen takes a trip to Lincoln with a friend called Joyce "We went into one shop and I managed to get just the white coronet I wanted, Joyce kept fitting them all on until we found the nicest." The pink spotted net is a problem, however. David asks a friend in the forces, Barbara, if she can keep a lookout. "She tried a number of shops and the only thing she saw was black net which was 13/6d per yard. She says if you did manage to get some, it would be very expensive." He puts feelers out in a number of directions. "About pink spotted net – Bob Rowley tells me that he and Joyce saw loads of it in the Lincoln market on Wed and Thurs this week at about 5/- to 6/- per yard. I am surprised Joyce did not get some for you." Eileen's aunts try for pink spotted net in Southport, London and Hastings, all to no avail, so in the end she settles for plain pink at 5/6d per yard. "Although it's not quite so pretty, it's a good match and I should hate to have left Helena out." She plans to have 3 bridesmaids – her own sister Dulcie and David's sisters Mary and Helena.

The honeymoon plans are taking shape and it is interesting to see how much is done via personal recommendation

> "We have a corporal, who used to be a Boots chemist – which gives you an idea of the type of place he is used to – well, he and his wife stayed at an address in Ilfracombe last year and he has

> passed it on to me. The lady can only take two lots of visitors at a time, so it is not crowded. He says they have a greengrocer's shop and there was never any shortage of salads and eggs for meals. He tells me she usually takes you on the terms 1) Bed and breakfast and 2) Evening meal. This enables you to have a whole day away and you can have lunch out or else she will willingly pack up sandwiches for a picnic. There is no formality about the place."

Someone else tries to put him off Ilfracombe saying it is "tremendously expensive and extortionate and any hotel would be eight guineas a week each!", but David sticks with the idea because of its good public transport links. One realises that it was not easy to obtain information on places that were further afield. Hence David writes to the Town Council for a booklet.

The distance to Devon was not going to be easily doable after the reception in Licolnshire and they hit on the idea of staying overnight in the cottage belonging to Mrs Lanc's mother in Limpsfield. "Mutti seems quite thrilled we should want to go there, she says she feels sure Mrs Turney would be agreeable and also that she would – in Mutti's words - 'Be a sport and let us have the cottage on our own'." So much seems to be arranged via personal contact rather than official routes and obviously cost came into it.

Unfortunately, the landlady in Ilfracombe turns out to be full up, so David is thrown back on the pamphlet from the Town council and then writes to 2 hotels and 3 boarding houses. Eileen is becoming ever more decisive because time is going by quite fast "I think if you should get the chance of suitable accommodation, you should book it straightaway, without waiting to write to me."

She is also still hankering after the pink spotted lace, having heard it is available in Lincoln market. "I really want to see it for myself to know whether it's really worth getting it and I also thought I would try to effect a part-exchange with the plain net. It's Friday 13th tomorrow, but I hope I'm lucky!" Later she writes: "I'm very glad I was able to get it because it means Helena won't feel at all self-conscious now as her dress will be identical with Mary's and Dulcie's."

She is delighted when she hears that accommodation has been booked with one of the boarding houses, "I'm confident we shall enjoy staying at a homely house rather than in a very big, formal hotel, where probably all the young people would be the gay 'cocktail' type, which neither of us like. Besides, it would be very foolish to pay £8. 8/- a week each for accommodation because we should feel that we ought not to spend so much on excursions to the surrounding places. I think you have done very well to get it all fixed up and it's certainly been a great help being able to ask the advice of the boys at camp." The actual cost was to be 3½ – 4 guineas per week. Although not physically well, her mother is also making various plans for the wedding. "She has found out it is possible to hire crockery from a shop in the village and also we shall be able to hire chairs from the Sunday school room." A taxi firm is to be booked and the Rev. Pawson (who was David's old C of E minister from childhood) has kindly agreed to perform the ceremony. Eileen is counting down the days "a mere 97 days now!!." A wedding ring is the next item on the agenda plus sorting out a wedding list and best man.

In the background, though, is a war. By April many rumours are running around the camp and no one is quite sure what the future holds. "The policy regarding the RAF has been published today and a 1/3rd are to be discharged in 12 months. Of the remaining 2/3rds it looks very much that I shall be in the 60% that are to be in British (or European) bases – the other 40% go to the Far East." Regrading on medical grounds because of his ear problems would render him in the 60% category. A Ministry of Labour official visits the base to explain about Demobilisation and Readjustment of sevicemen and the various Acts of Parliament governing it all. Each man had to fill in a form about his post-war aims "whether we had a job to go back to, what we did before the war and what we expected in the way of instruction in the Educational scheme. I just put down Civil Service Reconstruction Exams, because I expect to have got started on my course before the RAF do anything."

Thoughts of seaside and war become all intermingled, as David recounts what some of the boys at camp have told him about Ilfracombe and where they will be staying in Montpelier Terrace "There is nothing between the fronts of the houses and the sea view. You also <u>look down</u> on Capstone hill and the town. When you are in the rooms and planes fly about fairly low and dive down on the town and boy, you have the unusual experience of seeing them pass the window and you look down on them from above. It's most extraordinary until you get used to it!"

Return to Warboys, 29 January 1945

His cousin Derek from Manchester has agreed to be best man and has promised wooden fruit bowls as a wedding present. David is trying to smarten up with his clothes "On a clothing parade tonight I got some new trousers and a so-called new tunic which I fear is second hand. I shall get my other good tunic pressed this week and put it away until the date."

Eileen is perturbed to find that the white net which has been bought for her veil is shop-soiled, but her mother-in-law to be marches back to the shop and

David in the Radio Bunker at Warboys

manages to get it changed. Each of them want to look their absolute best, if possible. She is advised to have a wedding ring which is slightly smaller than her engagement ring "because I should be wearing it always and in soapy water it would need to fit tighter." It may be that only 9 carat utility wedding rings are available as new or possibly 18 or 22 carat as secondhand. Secondhand garments are acceptable, but a ring is different. She writes "Tonight I have been busy altering the white underslip which has been lent to me to wear under my wedding dress, that's another job done!"

By the end of April 1945 "the blackout restrictions here are raised entirely tonight! – I never did expect this on a military camp, but I suppose that now, when Jerry comes over, he will bomb the blacked out places only!" Around this same time Roosevelt dies. David comments "What sad news about Roosevelt, isn't it? We seem to have come to know and depend on him almost as much as one of our own statesmen, and it is unfortunate he will not see the finale to all his good work." On 1st May Eileen writes: "Isn't the war news marvellous? Events seem to be moving so quickly that anything might happen at any moment, it's most heartening to watch Fascism crumbling and dying out in Germany and Italy both at the same time; it can't be many more days to peace now – it will be almost unbelievable to realise that all the untold horrors will be at an end then." A week later there is a sense that something momentous is about to happen. She writes "I came home early from the office tonight because I had heard that Churchill was going to make his VE Day announcement at 6.0p.m.,

Return to Warboys, 29 January 1945

however it appears there are only unconfirmed reports of the capitulation, although all the agreements appear to have been signed. I'm sure the next few hours should bring the official declaration. There were quite a lot of flags out in Louth tonight and people seemed to be excited in a calm, quiet sort of way." The letter is then interrupted by an entry:

> "Tues morning V.E.DAY!!! I went to see Mr Bowder because it wasn't quite clear whether we should have to go to the office until 3.0p.m. today, the time of Churchill's announcement. However, he said he was going down to the office at 8.00 a.m. and I could ring him up, to know the position. He soon told me this morning that no-one had turned up, so I decided to pop home on the 9.33 a.m. and will be in Billingborough by 12.12 p.m. I wonder what celebrations you will be having in camp today. I do hope you don't have too many guards to do. I kept thinking how lovely it would be if you could come to Billingborough and this really is a great day for us, darling, because it means we shall be getting married in peacetime as we always wanted to. I do feel that we are very lucky in our plans."

David writes on the same day

> "It seems such a momentous day – one on which I must write to you and yet I hardly know what to say or how to start. I can hardly believe the war is over – it is such a difficult thing to imagine – but chiefly I see it as a fresh start for everyone – a chance to make something worthwhile of the world – and above all, the dawning of a new life

Return to Warboys, 29 January 1945

for the two of us. It is as if this great relief has come like a glimmer of dawn - the first light of a summer morning, and in a few weeks from now the dawn will break entirely for us both. That is how I see the end of the war - although I realise all this killing, fear and dark terror, which is so remote to us here, is over in Europe, and that England stands as firm as ever. I never fail to look at the lovely green fields and woods and enjoy them more these last few years. Today we had to go up to our sections at 9.0a.m. and at 10.30 a.m. the station Commander gave a short stand-down address, telling us we were free for today and tomorrow, but cannot go outside the district. We are all to have 48 hours Victory leave to be taken in the next 8 weeks. At 11.0 a.m. we had a Thanksgiving service taken in the open air by two Padres and now we are free.

Last night we went to the Pathfinders' demonstration – leaving Warboys at 7.0p.m. we went in an open air bus to Newmarket, where we stopped for 'jollities' and then carried on to the bombing range in the heart of most desolate Norfolk – somewhere near Thetford - about 70 miles from here. We reached there at 10.15 p.m. and there were crowds of airmen from all Pathfinder stations. The planes were from Warboys, loaded up with all the special sky markers and ground markers. We stood on a rising slope and about a mile away below us was a circle of lights which was the target. At 10.30 p.m. the first plane dropped a ground marker – a great red mountain of fire cascaded down and marked the ground about 20 yds from the target with a red patch of fire. Then came another – followed by skymarkers in green. These are balls of green fire suspended

Return to Warboys, 29 January 1945

> on small parachutes and are released in hundreds. They come down very slowly and make a brilliant light. Then a large green fire on a big parachute which kept firing red balls of fire downwards at intervals over the target. By 11.15p.m. the target was ready for the bombing and that is where we stopped short! I have never seen such a wonderful display before or such massive fireworks. We left there about 11.45 p.m. and were in here by 2.0 a.m. Some say a colour film was taken of the raid."

Eileen is equally excited about VE Day, but her experience is different, although it does involve 'fireworks' of a sort! She writes:

> "I think my V Day celebrations started when I reached Boston and found the town gaily decorated with flags and the centre of the place full of all kinds of Fairground amusements, there seemed to be hundreds of people standing about in groups, all on holiday, enjoying the news of Peace, everyone was very friendly and ready for a joke. I got home at 12.15p.m. and sprung a surprise on them all, they had laid a place for me for dinner, hoping that that would make me turn up. Norman had gunpowder all over the place manufacturing fireworks as fast as he could go. He made a Catherine wheel, Roman candle, red, white and blue and a rocket, he was in his element. On Tuesday afternoon we all listened to Churchill's announcement of Peace, it was a very historical and stirring speech, didn't you think so?
>
> Billingborough went very gay at night, they brought a piano out at the crossroads and held an impromptu dance, all the village and his wife came

Return to Warboys, 29 January 1945

out to join in the festivities, seats were placed along the pavements so even the old people were able to be there. We did the progressive barn dance, all the modern dances and then the Lancers, Larinka and so on; we all agreed that it must have been lovely when it was the usual thing to dance on the village green; it was such a friendly gathering and everyone thoroughly enjoyed it; it went on until midnight by the light of a floodlight on Wilson's shop. We went home at about 11.0p.m., had supper, put on our oldest clothes and went to light the huge bonfire in the field. Norman put the match to it just as Billingborough church struck twelve, at the same time the Land Girls' bonfire across near their hostel started, they both made a grand blaze. We had made Hitler out of a sack stuffed with straw, Norman put a bit of hair oil on his lock of hair to make him burn more fiercely; when the sticks underneath him gave way he did a header right into the heart of the fire, amid many cheers. The fireworks were very pretty inspite of the Catherine wheel losing its balance and refusing to spin round and the rocket getting anchored in its bottle! We all kept saying we wished you could have been there for all these celebrations; oh and we went to Horbling Church too, the church was packed and Mr Goshawk gave a nice informal talk. I came back to Louth on Wednesday. Louth Parish Church looked lovely last night, it had 4 searchlights playing up and down the spire, it looked like a silver dagger in the sky and could be seen from right down in the Marsh."

The war was over, but not everyone had escaped unscathed. Eileen mentions 'Dulcie's wounded airman' who came over from Rauceby Hospital on V Day afternoon.

> "He looked very weak, having only been out of bed since Saturday, he has been in hospital a year altogether and has had four operations. He told us that he is a Fitter and when working on a back turret of a plane, he got crushed under the wheel. He seemed to enjoy the change (of visiting us) as he hadn't been out for so long and he liked the milk and eggs Mummy gave him; we just let him sit around the house and in the garden, because he looked so worn out; he went back on the 6.40 bus and he had to walk 1½ mls from Sleaford towards Rauceby before he got a lift, his Surgeon finally picked him up in his car and teased him, saying he walked like an old man. He did an imitation of him in the ward the next morning."

With the ending of the war, some restrictions are being lifted. The basic ration of petrol will be on by the time of the wedding on 21st July which should ease the transport difficulties. Eileen is still counting the days — only 72 — and is now ready to see the local vicar about the banns. She only hopes he will not mind the vicar from Barnsley 'conducting' the ceremony and plans to get round this delicately by using the word 'assisting' instead. She also wants to ask if David's father can be allowed to play the organ and whether the church bells can be rung. It appears that this is all in order, but the bells will cost 30/- (5/- each ringer).

Having been ground based for all of the war, now in peacetime David eventually gets airborne! On 16th May he writes:

Return to Warboys, 29 January 1945

"I am feeling on top of the world, for an hour ago I got back from my first flight. There were five of us went on an air-test in 'T' for Tommy – Roy and George in the turrets and Barbara, Daphne and I standing behind the pilot. We were up for 35 minutes and flew round Huntingdon, St Ives, Hemingford and then up through the clouds and we rode on the top of a snowy blanket for a long time. It was lovely – we cruised around at 3000 ft. After the first few minutes I went down into the bomb-aimer's position and lay on my tummy, watching fields and farms pass by. When we got back, we circled the aerodrome and it was very easy to pick out the sites and buildings. It is certainly a lovely sight and you have no idea of speed. I have no qualms now about going to Germany. I think I shall go on another air test next week and ride in the turrets to get even more confidence. None of us felt sick – rather the opposite – I longed for something to eat and got very thirsty. Our pilot was the C.O Group Captain Deane and he sat there so calmly - the whole business seemed so easy to him that you could not fail to trust him."

Although David has technically booked his wedding and honeymoon leave, there is a remote possibility he could get a sudden posting to Germany or a posting within the UK for which he would be recalled.

Despite these vague fears, dress fitting for Helena, the youngest bridesmaid, is arranged by a weekend visit of the Laws family to the Holland family. "She did look nice in it, I think she felt a bit strange walking very sedately in a long frock, when a few minutes before she had been sprawling about on roller skates." Eileen is pressing on with plans – trying to hire a marquee and

Return to Warboys, 29 January 1945

"travelling by bus to Saltfleet of all places and I have succeeded in buying a pair of white satin court shoes, they are just what I wanted and only cost 10/- and no coupons." Given that David's daily wage at this point is 8/3d, this seems quite a lot of money in relative terms. Her justification is that after the wedding "I shall have them dyed for dance shoes." Wedding stationery and cake boxes are the other issues to be sorted out. They are expecting about 70 guests in all.

Towards the end of May David is offered the chance to fly over Germany to witness the devastation caused by the war. He seems keen to take advantage of this offer, although it would be saddening, especially as he was keen on the German language and had a German penfriend before the war. Their route will take them mainly up the Rhine beyond Cologne. By the end of June David still has various practical things to sort out in time for the wedding. He writes in a rather serious vein:

> "There are two points which I want to mention.
> 1) About cider. Barbara thinks it is an excellent idea for toasts and says if 'champagne cider' is obtainable, it is even nicer. I have never heard of it myself.
> 2) Flowers for the wedding are my responsibility – could you arrange to get what flowers you want and let me have the bill. This arrangement would be better than leaving it to me. I would probably buy garlic in mistake."

Eileen is still waiting for formal permission that she can be released from the Civil Service - without this piece of paper, no Marriage Gratuity could be granted.

Return to Warboys, 29 January 1945

She concentrates on what can be done practically toward the celebrations and this includes bottling 5 lbs of strawberries. She also has to apply for a new ration book which will be valid from the day after the wedding, but apparently it will have to still be in her maiden name because a Marriage Certificate needs to be presented with the application. Some hotels would refuse admittance unless the husband's and wife's identity cards agreed with the coupons, but she is hoping the landlady will not be too strict on the rules. They need to take Ration books, emergency ration cards and the appropriate number of points – 6 per person per week. They also are advised to bring their own jam and to provide their own towels and soap.

The invitation cards are finally sent out by June 19th and Eileen sends one to David, adding "RSVP in the affirmative!!" at the bottom. David jokingly replies "I will try to be there." Various promises of wedding presents are coming in, including a dinner wagon from Mutti Lanc, engraved silver serviette rings from Mr Laws' (senior) directors, a hand-woven shopping basket from a blind person, a damask table cloth and 6 serviettes, a mustard pot, a pyrex dish and fruit spoons. The Louth office has collected £2 :10 and Eileen has been searching the town for a coffee table, but "they are very scarce. There is an octagonal one at Fytches £3 which I might buy."

Helena needs one more fitting of her bridesmaid dress, various 'billets' in the village have to be sorted out ready for guests needing to stay overnight and the marquee which has been reserved must be paid for. A bracelet is to be bought for Dulcie, as bridesmaid "silver or washed gold would be quite all right", but this is David's direct responsibility. He has got the wedding ring, which is a good fit, fortunately.

As regards wedding photographs, they seem to be relying on Mr Kirby (the Baptist minister from Bluntisham) to provide his services. He suddenly suggests "he could probably arrange a camera in the church and by means of a cotton, take a snap of the actual ceremony – but he would require the vicar's permission to take photos in church first." Eileen does make enquiries on this point, but "Rev. Sampey will not give permission for a photo to be taken in church, he maintains that it would be like turning it into a cinema show, the Bishop in any case would not allow it, and he has never heard of it being done - so that's that, I'm afraid."

By 14th July David has partly packed his trunk, but promises Eileen "There will be plenty of room for your things!" Interestingly, he has had to borrow a swimming costume from somebody in Louth and a "nice pair of trunks" from somebody else in Barnsley. His mother is:

> "bringing ½ lb of sugar and ½lb of tea to help out towards our tea when we all arrive on Friday. Mother will bring rations of bacon, tea, sugar and margarine for our breakfasts at the different houses on Saturday morning. ... Mother is giving me a tin of marmalade and I shall have a couple of weekend ration cards which I suggest we spend at Ilfracombe, so that we might have extra sugar, butter and margarine for use on our picnics. Mother does not think there will be much butter spare for all our sandwiches, and if we have some of our own, it will ease things out. If you take a small tin mug, we can keep it in that."

Return to Warboys, 29 January 1945

His letters take on a slightly imperious tone in the week before the big day. He starts by announcing "Here is the first of a series of bulletins I am going to issue each day at lunchtime!" There are instructions about bringing shoe cleaning equipment, black and brown, and information on the camera films which he has acquired. No detail is spared, it would seem.

A stag party is to be held in St.Ives "About 15 of the chaps are coming and it seems it is the recognised thing to treat them all to a drink and then we will probably go for fish and chips and to the dance." Eileen answers each and every point in order, coordinating complicated travelling arrangements for people arriving at different times who will need taxis to get out to the village. All the hype turns into a more reflective mood by the Thursday before the wedding. David writes:

> "This will be the last letter that I shall be addressing to Miss Holland. How soon shall I get used to your new name? I have been wondering this morning darling, how many letters we have written to each other? It has been a wonderful correspondence, and owing to conditions, a most firm part in the building of our lives together. I have saved all your letters dear and we must hope our prefabricated house will provide sufficient room to store them somewhere! I am able to tell you that the wedding will take place – as arranged – in spite of all my anxious moments, for in less than two hours I shall be out of this place and on my way."

Postscript

Mr. & Mrs. George Holland
request the pleasure of
the company of

___the   bridegroom___

at the marriage of their daughter

Margaret Eileen,

with

Mr. David B. Laws,

at St. Andrew's Church, Billingborough,

on Saturday, July 21st, 1945,

at 1 p.m.

Brookfield House,
Billingborough,
Sleaford, Lincolnshire.

R.S.V.P.
in the affirmative!!

21
Postscript

The wedding was a very happy, if rather rushed occasion. The ceremony started at 1.00 p.m. in the church at Billingborough and by 3.30 p.m. the happy couple had left for Limpsfield in Surrey as a stop-over on their way to Ilfracombe. The newspaper report gives a good description

> "Given away by her father, the bride wore a gown of white cloque, cut on classical lines, with train, long net veil, surmounted by a dainty coronet, and she carried a bouquet of pink rosebuds. She was attended by 3 bridesmaids who were attired in dresses of pink spotted net over silk cloth, ornamented with pink rosebuds to harmonise with the bride's bouquet, halo headdresses of pink net and rosebuds. Their shower bouquets consisted of sweet peas in pastel shades and trailing fern.
>
> The service was choral with the bridegroom's father at the organ for the singing of the hymns:

Postscript

'O Perfect Love', 'God be in my head' and Psalm 'I lift up mine eyes unto the hills'. When the happy couple left for their honeymoon in Devonshire, the bride was attired in a grey tailored costume with hat and accessories to correspond. A merry peal was rung on the bells of St. Andrew's church after the service in honour of the event. Amongst the many handsome gifts received was a silver coffee pot from the bride and bridegroom's colleagues at the Tax Office."

Postscript

Sadly all the photographs of their honeymoon were lost in the post following the developing by Mr Kirby, but they solved this problem by going on exactly the same holiday the following year and taking similar shots!

The war was technically over, but it took a long time for David to be demobbed. Eileen did go back to look after her mother, as planned, having given up her

Margaret Eileen Holland.

With

Mr. & Mrs. David B. Laws'

Compliments.

Brookfield House,   21st July,
Billingborough.   1945.

Postscript

Departing on honeymoon

permanent Civil Service position and she puts in for her Marriage Gratuity. David is sent to Atherstone in Warwickshire on a radar course in September 45, then to Carnaby nr Bridlington in October. Around this time he writes:

Postscript

Ilfracombe

"I am delighted to be able to tell you that I have received a postcard from Walter, dated 6.2.45!!

Here is his exact message: 'Dear David. Short greetings from vast Africa. Unfortunately I was captured by the French in 1944 in Italy. It was terrible, but I can't change it now. On anyway, I hope our personal relations won't suffer from this dreadful war. On the contrary I wish to get an opportunity of paying back my debt to you and your parents as soon as possible. Best wishes to you and your parents, Mary and Helena. Yours faithfully Walter 1, Geryville, Algeria, French North Africa.' I am so pleased he has written and the question of replying to him is being considered. We cannot yet write to Germany, and he may have moved from Africa, so the solution may be to write to the Swiss uncle."

Close to Christmas David is moved again, this time to Manston aerodrome, nr Ramsgate. He sounds quite despondent: "Here I am, feeling most deserted, lost in the swirling mists which spread clammily and coldly,

Postscript

over the bleak flat wastes of Thanet – this forgotten corner of England - one feels it might be bitten off by the hungry seas around and disappear for ever in the Channel. And yet somewhere is a dear little lass sitting round a fireside, who means all the world to me, and perhaps she is enshrouded in these cold mists and feels that Thanet is so far away too."

He spends another Christmas in camp, but is then granted leave for the New Year.

> "As a Xmas dinner it was good - but for the jollifications, the occasion lacked any spirit. There were only about 50 for dinner, no singing – not a patch on Warboys last year. I subsided onto my bed, later went to tea, which was only biscuits and cake standing round a table and played SNOOKER! All evening.
>
> So ended a rather aimless and lonely day. HOWEVER – on Boxing Day I went to Whitstable to some friends (whom I had not seen before) and had a good day at their bungalow which is right on the front about 20yds from the high tide mark. I had gin and lime as aperitif on arrival, pheasant with all the etceteras and Christmas pud with rum poured all over it, followed by walnuts and port and fruit. In the afternoon I had my slippers on, by the fire with a book full of dreadful picture jokes and for supper had another do with soup, more pheasant and so to bed at about 11.0 p.m."

22
Manston airfield, 1946

RAF life continues, but thoughts are on the life beyond demobilisation. Studying in earnest for the Civil Service executive grade exams involves writing essays on topics of general knowledge. Practising for this David says:

> "I am at the moment suffering from brain fog and writer's cramp. In the past 2 hours I have been doing a general knowledge test, writing non-stop nearly all the time and doing about 3000 words. Truly my brain feels as if it has been taken out, scrubbed with a stiff brush, rinsed and is now hanging up to dry in a much shrivelled state! The questions were good ones.
>
> I could have written heaps more, but had not time. Here they are:
>
> 1. What are the difficulties in British agriculture and how far is permanent prosperity possible?
> 2. How do you account for the average increase

> in the length of life in Britain?
> 3. Give some account of Britain's food during the war
> 4. What arguments occur to you for and against hire purchase systems."

These questions seem a bit strange to a 21st century ear, but will perhaps become relevant again in time with our ageing population, debt crises and coming out of the EU common agricultural policy.

David also had to do arithmetic practice papers and precis exercises, but he did not seem to find these a problem.

Letters in early January 1946 are dominated by medical and dental issues. David sounds to have contracted ringworm from some dirty blankets on the previous RAF camp. Having spent a week's leave in Barnsley with Eileen, he is concerned lest she should catch it and is obviously quite embarrassed about the diagnosis. He writes: "CONFIDENTIAL; In case you should be reading aloud, I have put this! I feel it is a duty to tell you something which may affect you, though it is difficult to write about. I went to see the M.O. this morning and he immediately diagnosed it as TINEA – a skin trouble which may be due to dirty blankets which I had at Honiley. He has ordered daily treatment of 'Whitfields' ointment for 5 days and then I must see him again. I feel so terribly sorry about this, darling, and hope you are not annoyed with me and I do hope you don't catch it. Perhaps you would look up in a book and forward me any information about it – it's the first time I have ever had any skin trouble in the RAF."

Manston airfield, 1946

Eileen, as ever practical, is not worried about this. She is more preoccupied with trying to buy a bed for them both in the future.

> "The other day I received 6 dockets from the Board of Trade, these will enable us to buy a mattress, two blankets and 3 sheets. I am going to look at some mattresses in Sleaford tomorrow, there is a very reliable furniture shop there. I may as well order one, as it will probably take quite a long time to come. I think a 'Slumberland' deep spring mattress would be nice, similar to the one which we had at Mrs Matthews (on honeymoon)."

In fact when she visits the shop, she is told that only one in twelve mattresses received are interior spring ones, but as her family are old customers and if they did not mind waiting, they could have a spring one. "There were 4 different qualities of these ranging from £10 - £14, the most expensive one was composed of wool hair and springs, while the others were of cotton felt and springs. I thought it wisest to order to best quality because the wool will be warmer and more comfortable than cotton. The dockets are all for Utility things so we can be sure we aren't paying excessively. It was quite fun doing this first bit of shopping, I felt quite important airing my views on house furnishing!"

However, she has still not received her Marriage Gratuity and David thinks she should write again to remind them there has been 4 months' delay. Eileen has put her name down for some new houses which are being built off Eastfield Road in Louth, but it is not clear whether these are prefabs or not. She is also getting into the role of a future housewife by attending evening cookery classes in Sleaford. "We learnt how to make brown stew, crunch, fishcakes and queen cakes." Another time she is taught how to make chocolate cakes and mutton stew.

The date of the Executive exam is announced on the wireless as being 2nd April, so the pressure is on to study as much as possible via the correspondence course. The next subjects tackled via essays are the Judiciary System and the Population problem – why the population is falling and the economic effects over a number of years and measures to increase it (theoretical and not practical). Unfortunately, the ringworm has not entirely cleared up and the treatment is changed to 'Castellani's paint', a vivid purple liquid containing a proportion of iodine.

> "It has the property of destroying old skin and encouraging new skin to grow. It dyes the skin a bright purple and is hard to wash off the fingers. With my lint and bandages, I have managed to keep most of the stuff off my clothes, but it has coloured my shirt and pants in parts. I wondered whether you would mind my sending them to you next Thursday to be boiled and washed <u>separately</u>? They might colour anything boiled with them! And the laundry might object."

What comes across in these letters of early married life is that they both have a very clearly defined view of the division of labour between male and female roles and are quite happy to accept this. David writes: "I was studying some photographs of these modern kitchens

Manston airfield, 1946

in pre-fabs and could just picture you busy in such ideal surroundings. I do hope we get a modern house and not an old one where you have to tolerate ancient washing and cooking appliances." He is quite happy to send her the allotment of 39/- per week which is presumably docked from his pay by the Forces. She in turn is quite happy to sign off her letters with "Ever your little wife who loves you very very much" or "Always your little missus."

They manage quite a few leaves together in February and March, but after each one they grow more and more restless and longing for the time to set up home together.

Eileen has plenty of work to do looking after her mother, who seems to suffer from frequent colds in the winter. Nonetheless, she likes to involve herself in the local community and is happy to take on running the Guides as an outside diversion. Sadly her grandmother in Liverpool becomes ill and dies in March, so this becomes another demand upon her, as she must attend the funeral as a family representative, because her mother is not fit enough to travel. She stays on for a couple of weeks in order to keep her aunts company and then returns to Lincolnshire.

She is trying to plan things, but it is hard to know where life will take them next:"I have opened an account at the Trustee Savings Bank in Sleaford and have replied to the A. and C.G. about the investment of the gratuity (£98.9.3d) I also enquired at the Labour Exchange about a job and they are going to let me know if a part-time vacancy occurs. I called to see Mr Smeeton about the furniture dockets. He advised us to put down for one of everything, because the dockets are not for specified

Manston airfield, 1946

David's German penfriend's parents, Herr and Frau Schweizer (on the right) pictured at Randen on the Swiss German border.

things and can be spent just as we wish. He says in any case we shall only get the maximum which is 60, but of which only 30 can be spent straightaway, the remaining 30 may not become valid for another year, depending on supplies. A bedroom suite takes 28 dockets!" The officer at the Labour Exchange said "there weren't many part-time jobs now, as employers will not be bothered with part-timers now that they can get demobbed people full-time."

As it happened David was, it seems, demobbed in May of 1946, and initially returned to Louth Tax office. They did not have a home of their own, but continued

Manston airfield, 1946

to lodge with Mr and Mrs Lanc. Eileen was responsible for doing the cleaning one week and the cooking the next.

All correspondence obviously ceased at this point until 1947 when David is sent to London as an Executive Officer in the Exchequer and Audit Dept and they are briefly separated again.

There is a sad card which arrives in May 1946 from his German penfriend, written in German "Dear David, Many thanks for your letter of 14.12.45 to my uncle. I am POW of the French. I am not allowed to write English. Otto (brother) is dead or POW in USSR?? I do not know anything of my parents since October 1945?? We were badly betrayed by the Nazis!! I am glad that this government is now gone. All the best to you, your parents, Mary and Helena."

This prompts David to write to the uncle in Switzerland to see if he can obtain more precise news of the family. On 21.6.46 a moving letter is received plus a couple of photos. Herr Egger writes:

> "The post with Germany is irregular and unreliable. On one occasion it failed altogether and then I was obliged to use other suggested ways to attain my objective. Now I can give you the news that we were able to carry out our long wished for meeting from Whit Sunday to Monday. You yourself can indeed imagine the joy it was for us four people. At first we were all so overcome that we looked at one another from head to foot and then after the first surprise, we shook hands, with sad hearts.
>
> Yes, yes dear English people, it is a sorry and

Manston airfield, 1946

bitter meeting after so long a time, when you are told of their sad life and misfortunes. However, throughout all their long silence I may assure you that Father and Mother Schweizer are in good health and that Otto is alive. Just a few days before Whitsun, they received a card from Russia, so we celebrated a real meeting. We were well treated by the people in Randen, for my brother-in-law said on Sunday 'Today let's have a wedding breakfast' and here is what this family put on our table: soup, fried ham, potatoes and salad – such things were unknown to the Schweizers since the beginning of the war. Unfortunately we were not allowed to give them the food we had with us, which made us very sorry for they were all things which would have done them good on their bare table. Every month they get 3 ½ ounces of fat or butter each and 2 ½ ozs of meat per week and 2 ¼ lbs of bread for two persons per week; and that is all. Shoes, stockings and socks are in short supply everywhere. Hitler and his followers have left behind an heirloom which the whole of Europe must endure for many a long year. But in my opinion there is no peace when a people are slowly and surely starving to death. There were thousands who always fought a bitter, silent battle against the Nazis, as indeed the whole Schweizer family did at all times, and now it is a fact that the authorities leave these secret fighters to fend for themselves and leave the Nazis with their 'run with the hare and hunt with the hounds attitude' in the leading official positions. I could write you a whole book about what the Schweizers told us and what not only they, but other people in Randen who live on the frontier told us, concerning this. I have naturally written to Walter as soon as possible

about our meeting and he will have quiet joy that
all is well."

In fact it took until 17th December 1947 for Walter to be released from being a prisoner of war. He had ended up in Lorraine in France after coming back from Algeria, but because he was not physically capable of working in a coal mine, he was released home to Germany.

And so a whole sorry period of history draws to a close. David and Eileen eventually moved in 1948 to a semi-detached house in Sidcup, Kent. My sister, Margaret, had been born in the March of that year and at last they were all able to be together in that 'home of their own' for which they had longed. Their marriage was a happy one, lasting 64 years and I am most grateful to them for all they have been as people and for all they have done for us as children.

www.ingramcontent.com/pod-product-compliance
Lightning Source LLC
Chambersburg PA
CBHW071225080526
44587CB00013BA/1507